ORIENTAL
BLUE AND WHITE

THE FABER MONOGRAPHS
ON POTTERY AND PORCELAIN

Former Editors: W. B. Honey *and* Arthur Lane

Present Editors: Sir Harry Garner *and* R. J. Charleston

A. FIRST HALF, FOURTEENTH CENTURY. HT. 11.1 in.
Japanese Collection
See page xxvi

ORIENTAL
BLUE AND WHITE

by

SIR HARRY GARNER

FABER AND FABER
London

First published in 1954
by Faber and Faber Limited
24 Russell Square London W.C.1
Second edition 1964
Third edition 1970
Printed in Great Britain by
Latimer Trend and Company Limited
Whitstable
Colour plates printed by
Fine Art Engravers Limited, Godalming

SBN 571 04702 5

To

IVY CLARK

Whose lovely collection of early Chinese blue
and white, formed jointly by her late husband
ALFRED CLARK and herself, has given
pleasure and inspiration to many.

FOREWORD

Painting on porcelain in underglaze cobalt blue making what we call 'blue and white' has been the most widespread of all forms of ceramic decoration. Its history is inseparably linked with Chinese porcelain of the Ming period; and its first great vogue dates from the fourteenth century when 'blue and white' began to be exported from China in quantity. Then too began its imitation in other ceramic materials in the Near East, whence the fashion spread eventually to Europe.

The fashion still holds while controversy continues. Sir Harry Garner here studies first the fourteenth century wares, about which a great deal has been learned recently from the great collections at Teheran and Istanbul, with many new observations, and then the classical wares of the fifteenth century, differentiating the styles of the several reigns and illustrating many newly discovered specimens. But by no means all are of merely documentary interest. Many are masterpieces of familiar types including Corean wares and even some little-known examples from Japan and Indo-China.

The book is illustrated by a hundred plates of which four are in colour.

W. B. H.

CONTENTS

ILLUSTRATIONS

Where no collection is named for a piece illustrated, the piece is
from the author's collection.

PREFACE TO THE
THIRD EDITION

Five years have passed since the second edition of *Oriental Blue and White* was published, and once again it is necessary for a reassessment to be made of the original text, written more than fifteen years ago, taking into account the large amount of new information that has come to light in recent years. Most of this has come from the export wares; little, unfortunately, has come from China itself. Extensive archaeological excavations of kiln sites and tombs in China have thrown much light on the ceramics of the earlier periods. But it has not been possible for excavations to be made in the Ching-tê Chên area where most of the blue and white porcelain was manufactured, and the practice of burying treasured objects in tombs had declined greatly by the thirteenth and fourteenth centuries, so that little information has come from this source.

Perhaps the most important point in the study of the blue and white wares, on which there is still much speculation, is the origin of the wares. The brief account, given in Chapter 2, p. 9, of how blue and white was derived from the *ch'ing-pai* and *shu fu* white porcelains still seems to be generally sound, but there is no doubt that the subject is more complex than as it is presented there. The forthcoming book by Miss Margaret Medley on the ceramics of the Yüan dynasty will without doubt throw further light on the origins of blue and white, as one of the most important aspects in the development of Yüan ceramics.

The view, expressed in 1954, that blue and white porcelain was first made in China near the beginning of the fourteenth century does not seem to have been upset in any way since then. Suggestions, based largely on archaeological and scientific evidence, have been made from time to time that blue and white may have been first made some thirty or more years earlier, which would bring its origin into the Sung dynasty. But the evidence produced so far is not sufficiently precise to fix a date within such a close period as thirty years. In particular, the evidence from the Carbon 14 method requires close scrutiny; there has been a tendency to stretch the evidence far beyond the bounds defined by strict scientific principles.

The question of an error of a mere thirty years in dating is in itself of little importance. The larger issue is whether the new technique of painting under the glaze was introduced from the west by the Mongols or was a native innovation. The evidence that it came from outside is overwhelming. In the original text of *Oriental Blue and White* perhaps the major criticism which could be raised today is that full justice was not done to the tremendous impact of the Mongols on ceramic development during the Yüan dynasty. This is demonstrated, not only by the blossoming of decoration in blue and white to become, in a few decades, one of the most important achievements in the whole of ceramic history, but by other developments as well. The piece that has provided, more than any other, evidence of the restless aspirations of the Yüan potters for something entirely new is the so-called Gaignières-Fonthill vase, in which no fewer than four distinct techniques of decoration have been applied to a single piece of white porcelain. The history of this fascinating piece was fully explored by Arthur Lane,[1] from its first appearance in Europe in the fourteenth century, where it was fitted with sumptuous silver-gilt enamel mounts, through its various vicissitudes, during which it appeared in the collections of various owners and disappeared into obscurity a number of times, down to its final rediscovery eight years ago in the National Museum of Ireland, Dublin, robbed of its precious mounts, which are now lost. Lane gives strong reasons for ascribing the vase to *circa* 1300 and there are equally strong reasons for thinking, as he did, that the introduction of painting in underglaze blue, derived from cobalt and underglaze red, derived from copper, occurred at about the same time.[2] Many other innovations in ceramic technique were introduced in the early fourteenth century, which reveal the Yüan dynasty as one of the most enterprising in Chinese ceramics. The paper given by John Ayers to the Oriental Ceramic Society in 1956 on Yüan ceramics[3] shows the wide range of types covered in this short dynasty. Many of the types left their mark on the later developments of the Ming dynasty, but by the end of the fourteenth century painting in underglaze blue had far outstripped the rival techniques and it became, from then on, the dominant method of decoration of Chinese porcelain up to the eighteenth century. The study of the development of all the types and their

[1] Arthur Lane, 'The Gaignières-Fonthill vase: A Chinese porcelain of about 1300', *The Burlington Magazine*, CIII, April 1961, pp. 124–32.

[2] The view now held by some experts is that the date of introduction of painting in underglaze blue was *circa* 1320 rather than 1300.

[3] John Ayers, 'Some characteristic wares of the Yüan dynasty', *Transactions of the Oriental Ceramic Society*, Vol. 29, 1954–55, pp. 69–83.

relationship to blue and white, fascinating as it is, must be regarded as falling outside the scope of this book.

The study of blue and white has long been bedevilled by attempts to reconcile the conflicting references to it in the Chinese literature. Sir Percival David was the pioneer among western authorities in giving critical consideration to the Chinese texts on ceramics, first in exposing the fradulent album of Hsiang[1] and then by his exhaustive treatment of all the texts dealing with Ju porcelain,[2] which has a wide application to Chinese ceramics in general. John Pope has given an admirable analysis of the literature on blue and white[3] and has repeated Sir Percival David's warning about the 'uncritical and almost indiscriminate acceptance of the various texts'. It ought not therefore to be necessary to go further into this question. But the importance of the origins and early history of blue and white makes it desirable to look in some detail at the references on the sources of cobalt, which have an important bearing on the history and dating of these wares.

All the early writers in the west on blue and white, from Bushell onwards, have been obsessed with the problem of identification of 'Mohammedan blue', the cobalt ore imported into China from Islamic countries, and with attempts to identify pieces of blue and white in which it was used. This is not surprising. The *T'ao Shuo*,[4] for long regarded by connoisseurs as the bible of Chinese ceramics, is full of references to it in its various forms, *hui-hui-ch'ing*, *su-ni-p'o* and *su-ma-ni*. The admiration accorded to the beautiful blue colour produced by the imported ore is little short of veneration. There are many references to its rarity and the periods during which it was available in the Ming dynasty. It is a shock to find, on close examination, that there is no reference to 'Mohammedan blue', in any of its forms, earlier than the end of the sixteenth century. It is not surprising that early western writers, with little but export porcelain of the sixteenth century to guide them, should have gone so badly astray in their over-confidence in the references to 'Mohammedan blue'.

A re-reading of the original text of *Oriental Blue and White* shows it to be not entirely free from over-reliance on the *T'ao Shuo*, but one piece of evidence, not from this work, is quoted which should at least

[1] Sir Percival David, 'Hsiang and his album', *Transactions of the Oriental Ceramic Society*, Vol. 11, 1933–34, pp. 22–47.

[2] Sir Percival David, 'A commentary on Ju ware', *Transactions of the Oriental Ceramic Society*, Vol. 14, 1936–37, pp. 18–69.

[3] John Alexander Pope, *Chinese Porcelains from the Ardebil Shrine*, pp. 27–33.

[4] S. W. Bushell, *Description of Chinese Pottery and Porcelain, being a Translation of the T'ao Shuo*, 1910.

have been reliable. On p. 15 there is a reference to the *Ming Annals*, stating that *hui-hui-ch'ing* was brought as tribute from Sumatra to China in the years 1426, 1430, 1433 and 1434. This information was derived from Hobson,[1] who probably based his statement on Groeneveldt.[2] In fact Sumatra, or, to be more precise, Acheh (North-West Sumatra), is mentioned in the *Ming Annals* for the second year of Yung-lo (1404) as paying tribute to China. From then onwards there are many more references to tribute being paid, including those for the years mentioned by Hobson, but they do not mention *hui-hui-ch'ing*.

Amidst all this confusion, we now have positive evidence for the first time on the cobalt ore used in the early manufacture of blue and white. This comes from scientific analyses made by the Archaeological Research Laboratory, Oxford, in 1955. The work was done after the first edition of *Oriental Blue and White* was published, but some reference to the analyses should have been made in the second edition. More recent tests, published in 1967, have helped to confirm the earlier tests and have extended them to a still wider field. The results of the combined tests show that all the fourteenth-century pieces examined were made from imported ore and suggest that native ore was not used in China before the fourth decade of the fifteenth century.

To understand how these conclusions were reached it is necessary to know in what forms cobalt occurs in nature. There are two main types of cobalt ore. One is a mixture of oxides of cobalt and manganese and the other is a compound oxide of cobalt and arsenic. The former occurs as asbolite, an unattractive amorphous dark grey mineral. The latter occurs mainly in two forms, erythrite and cobaltite. Erythrite is a beautiful pink crystalline material and cobaltite is formed of black crystals with a metallic sheen. These two forms are found in Persia and are described in detail by Abulqasim ifm Abdullah, a potter of Kashan, in a manuscript dated A.D. 1301.[3] He refers to asbolite as being brought from the land of the Franks, i.e. Europe.

Cobalt was first used as a colouring agent, not in ceramics but in glass. The earliest blue glass was made in the Mesopotamian valley round about 2000 B.C. and there can be no doubt that the cobalt was of Persian origin, probably erythrite from Khemsar, about 120 miles south of Tehran, where it could be found, until recent times, in the

---

[1] R. L. Hobson, *The Wares of the Ming Dynasty*, 1924, p. 53.

[2] W. P. Groeneveldt, *Verhandelingen van het Bataviaasch Genootschap en Wetenschappen*, Vol. XXXIX, 1877, p. 92.

[3] Published and translated in an article in *Orientalische Steinbucher und Persiche Fayencetechnik* by H. Ritter, J. Ruske, F. Sarre and R. Winderlich, Istanbul, 1935.

form of flower-like masses growing, as it were, on the surface. This attractive mineral must have intrigued the early craftsmen and we need not be surprised at its exploitation as a colouring agent at a very early date.

The first ceramic wares in which cobalt is known to have been used were the tin-glazed earthenwares of Mesopotamia, first made in the ninth century A.D.[1] They were painted with designs in blue, sometimes with the addition of green, derived from copper, applied over the glaze. In the late twelfth century the potters of Kashan went a stage further by painting designs in blue under the glaze. The erythrite at Khemsar was handy, only twenty miles away.

Cobalt today is one of the most important metals in industry. Used for four thousand years entirely for its decorative qualities, it is now used in the manufacture of high grade steels and nuclear power plants. As a result of its importance in modern industry, a thorough survey has been made of its distribution all over the world. One result of this survey is to establish that the only form of cobalt ore to be found in China is asbolite. Thus the absence of manganese in cobalt decoration in Chinese ceramics is a certain indication that imported ores were used in the manufacture.

The series of analyses made at Oxford in 1955 were planned to throw some light on the kind of ore used in the manufacture of early Chinese blue and white.[2,3] The pieces included nine of fourteenth-century date as well as fifteen attributed to the fifteenth century. Representative groups of sixteenth-, seventeenth- and eighteenth-century pieces were also included.

The most important result of these tests was to show that every fourteenth-century piece was free from manganese, so that all the pieces were made with imported ore. There was not sufficient evidence to determine precisely when native ore was first used, but it was certainly in the fifteenth century and probably during the second quarter.

In the more recent tests of 1967, further analyses of a large number of pieces of blue and white, including some fourteenth- and fifteenth-century examples, were made.[4] An improved method of analysis was used for these tests. It is not easy to make a precise quantitative

[1] Arthur Lane, *Early Islamic Pottery*, 1951.

[2] Stuart Young, 'An analysis of Chinese blue and white', *Oriental Art*, Vol. II, No. 2, 1956, pp. 43–47.

[3] Sir Harry Garner, 'The use of imported and native cobalt in Chinese blue and white', *Oriental Art*, Vol. II, No. 2, 1956, pp. 48–50.

[4] M. S. Banks and J. M. Merrick, 'Further analysis of Chinese blue and white', *Archaeometry*, Vol. 10, 1967.

comparison of the two series of tests, but the main conclusions reached on the earlier tests were fully endorsed. The four fourteenth-century pieces and the six attributed to the early fifteenth century included in the second series of tests were all found to be made from imported ore.

The picture that emerges from the facts given above is that the use of underglaze blue was a Persian invention of the late twelfth century, that the technique and the Persian cobalt ore were brought to China about one hundred years later, and that this imported ore was used for another 100 years before the Chinese, having discovered their own sources of supply, began to use the native cobalt.

But it must be said that the decoration in Chinese blue and white, as generally understood, owes little to the Persian underglaze blue. The blue in the Kashan wares, brilliant in colour, tends to run badly and it was only used to produce broad effects. The Persian potters were very well able to produce fluent designs with the brush under the glaze but they were confined, in the Kashan wares, to designs in black. The reason for the running of the cobalt in the Persian earthenwares is not at present completely understood. Running does not occur, to any large extent, in the early Chinese blue and white, although it is recorded that later on (see pp. 15, 16), the Chinese potters sometimes added native to the imported ore to prevent the blue from running.

The designs of the early blue and white wares introduced new elements to Chinese art and the question of how much they owe to foreign influence is largely unexplored. Certainly the designs have little connection with those of contemporary Persian ceramics and parallels must be sought in other fields such as metalwork. But, although the stylistic connections with the art of Persia and other West-Asian countries are at present tenuous, we cannot escape the feeling that the impact of the Mongol invasion on the whole of Chinese art was enormous.[1] It seems that a new breath of life was brought to the decaying art of the late Sung dynasty, isolated for so long from outside communication. The exuberance of the blue and white of the fourteenth century, as different from the restrained designs of Sung ceramics as it is from the later carefully controlled imperial blue and white of the fifteenth century, is one facet of the impact of the Mongols.

Before we leave the question of the composition of the cobalt ores, it is worth while saying more about the date at which the native ore came into general use. As I have said, the scientific evidence is not sufficient at present to determine this date accurately. But the results

[1] See *Chinese Art under the Mongols: the Yüan Dynasty (1279–1368)*, 1968, and in particular Sherman Lee's introduction, pp. 22, 23.

already obtained suggest that cobalt analysis, combined with other scientific work, may provide a powerful means of dating certain types of fifteenth-century blue and white.

In the preface to the second edition of this book I referred to the attempt made by Miss Margaret Medley to regroup fifteenth-century blue and white on the basis of the structure of the glaze. Progress on this subject has not been very rapid since the original experiments were made in 1963, but we shall no doubt see a slow and steady progress in the elucidation of the problem. It is worth recording, however, that since the paper was written we have seen, almost without a murmur, general acceptance of the view that the 'stepped base' group, often bearing the Hsüan-tê mark, can be dated to the inter-regnum period (1436–1464).

We find from the two sets of cobalt analyses that every piece with the Hsüan-tê mark that was tested, twenty-six in all, was made with some admixture of the native ore, while unmarked pieces attributed to the early part of the fifteenth century were generally made with imported ore. One possible interpretation of these facts is that the introduction of the native ore took place before the Hsüan-tê period. But there is another possibility, that the introduction of native cobalt took place later and that the marked pieces are later than the marks indicate. A fair proportion of the marked pieces belong to the stepped base group, now generally accepted as belonging to the inter-regnum period. Strong arguments could be produced to support a similar attribution for many of the remaining pieces, but we need more evidence before the question is finally settled.

The acceptance of the stepped base group and some other pieces with the Hsüan-tê mark as belonging to the inter-regnum period has been long overdue. I suggested in the first edition of this book (p. 24) that it was against all reason to ascribe a large proportion of fifteenth-century blue and white to such a short period as the nine years of the reign of Hsüan-tê, leaving virtually nothing to the thirty years of the inter-regnum period.[1] But I did not then expect to find such a large group requiring to be transferred as I do now. I should not be surprised if the studies of the next few years resulted in the transfer of most of the pieces bearing the Hsüan-tê mark to the once despised inter-regnum period, which will surely in the future occupy a distinguished place in the history of Chinese blue and white.

Nine pieces with the Ch'êng-hua mark were included in the second set of tests. It may be said that none of the recent scientific work

[1] John Pope had independently come to the same conclusion. See *Chinese Porcelains from the Ardebil Shrine*, pp. 102–103.

throws any doubt on the attribution of pieces of this group to the period of the mark. All the pieces tested were made with native mixed with imported cobalt except one, which was made almost entirely with imported ore. The differences in quality, in glaze and colour, between the Ch'êng-hua and earlier blue and white was well known to Chinese connoisseurs and this no doubt led to the conclusion reached by some Chinese writers that it was during the Ch'êng-hua reign that the supply of imported ore failed.[1] We know now that the introduction of the native ore took place some time before this.

At this stage we should mention the types of blue and white that were exported to South-East Asia, including Malaya, Indonesia and the Philippines. The large amount of material excavated in recent years,[2] especially in the Philippines, includes a number of different types of blue and white, some of which were certainly made in Ching-tê Chên and some of which, including the so-called Annamese wares, were not. We still do not know where these Annamese wares were made, nor can we date them exactly, but we may be certain that some of them belong to the fifteenth century. Another distinct group came from the province of Fukien. Here again the dating of Fukien blue and white is uncertain, although we know that the manufacture of the so-called 'Swatow wares', named after the port from which they were shipped, was well established in the second half of the sixteenth century. One great value of the controlled Philippines excavations is that they should give reliable information on the relative dating of the different groups, which will enable us to determine the dates of the Annamese and Fukien groups of blue and white by comparison with contemporary Ching-tê Chên wares, which can be otherwise dated. A feature of the ceramic wares exported to South-East Asia in all categories, including blue and white, is that they include many small pieces, whose functions are not always evident. Moreover, they include types that were not exported to Western Asia, nor are they to be found, as far as our present evidence goes, in China itself. The

---

[1] See, for example, the *Tsun-chêng pa-chien*, by Kao Lien, published in 1591. This work is not specifically mentioned in the *T'ao Shuo* (although it appears to be in mind on p. 59), but it is referred to by Brankston, *Early Ming Wares of Ching-techen*, pp. 40, 89. In fact, the composition of the cobalt in Ch'êng-hua blue and white shows that there was no failure in the supply of the imported ore. A relative scarcity may have occurred, but it is more likely that a mixture of native and imported ore was deliberately chosen to produce the soft blue tones that were so popular in the Ch'êng-hua period, not only in the blue and white, but also in the *tou-ts'ai* wares.

[2] The recently published book by Leandro and Cecilia Locsin, *Oriental Ceramics discovered in the Philippines*, 1967, describes the most important controlled excavations made so far of the eastern export wares.

great amount of field work being undertaken at present, especially in the Philippines, may be expected to produce a great advance in knowledge of these new types during the next few years.

As for the Chinese sixteenth-century blue and white wares made in Ching-tê Chên, difficulties of the kind that beset us in the blue and white of the fifteenth century do not arise. The official porcelains of the Chêng-tê, Chia-ching, Lung-ch'ing and Wan-li periods present few problems. The blue and white exported to Europe and Western Asia in the sixteenth century, which were typical of the wares made for home consumption of all but the wealthiest classes in China, are well represented in western collections, of which that in the Topkapu Sarayi in Istanbul is outstanding. These collections have been so well studied in the past that there seems to be little fresh to learn about them. It is not until we get to the third decade of the seventeenth century that it becomes necessary to add some new information to what was said in the first edition of this book.

The so-called 'transition wares', a term loosely applied to the wares of the period from 1620 to 1662 (sometimes extended to 1683), form one of the most attractive and interesting groups of Chinese blue and white. To the western connoisseur the term is generally applied to the finely painted wares decorated with landscapes, sometimes with the addition of human or animal figures, growing plants, flowers or floral scrolls (Plates 60–63, Colour Plate F), which were exported in large numbers to Europe. Until the present century they adorned country houses in England, Holland and other countries, neglected by the avid nineteenth-century collectors of K'ang-hsi blue and white, who must have ransacked every promising source in the search for 'prunus jars' and similar types. It was not until the 1930s that the transition wares began to be appreciated, largely as the result of the activities of a small group of English collectors who were attracted by the fine quality of the porcelain, the beautiful violet-blue of the decoration and above all by the splendid brushwork, which seems to reflect the spirit of the landscape painting of the period. Today the transition wares are held in high regard. It is convenient, to avoid confusion later, to refer to these wares as 'western transition wares', to distinguish them from the 'eastern transition wares', which travelled eastwards to Japan.

The transition wares that reached Japan in the same period are entirely different from those familiar to the west. They can be divided into two main groups, the roughly finished pieces known as *ko-sometsuke*, 'old blue and white', made mostly in the T'ien-ch'i period (1621–1627) and the first half of the Ch'ung-chêng period

(1628–1643), and the pieces of much finer quality known as the Shonzui wares, which were made somewhat later, but which overlapped the *ko-sometsuke* wares in the reign of Ch'ung-chêng.[1] Both types were used in the Tea Ceremony and the Japanese terms are those given by the Tea Masters.

The *ko-sometsuke* wares seem to have been made largely and the Shonsui wares entirely for export. They are almost unknown in China today and there are none in the Chinese Imperial Collections. Until recently, when a number of *ko-sometsuke* wares, generally dishes in sets of five, decorated in underglaze blue, sometimes with touches of decoration in red, green and yellow enamels, were released from Japan as a result of the decline in popularity of the Tea Ceremony, they were virtually unknown in western countries as well.

The *ko-sometsuke* wares are coarse in quality, both in the porcelain and the glaze, which breaks away from the thin edges. The chipped edges are described by the Japanese as *mushikui*, 'moth-eaten'. There are often accretions of sand on the base and round the foot-rim, rather like those found on the Swatow wares. The blue of the decoration is dull greyish in tone. In spite of all these defects, the *ko-sometsuke* wares are greatly admired in Japan for the freedom and vitality of the designs, generally confined to simple landscapes or growing plants. A typical piece is shown in Colour Plate G. Japanese writers have criticised western connoisseurs and collectors because of their lack of taste in 'preferring the overpowering porcelain of the Ming and Ch'ing dynasties from government kilns' to the more beautiful *ko-sometsuke* wares.[2]

There could be no greater contrast than that between the *ko-sometsuke* and Shonzui wares. The porcelain of the Shonzui wares is of fine quality, carefully finished and painted in a refined cobalt-blue not unlike that used in the 'western transition wares'. The decoration, in contrast with the sparse and sketchy painting of the *ko-sometsuke* wares, is highly sophisticated and even over-crowded. The designs are often broken up into formal panels, with brocade borders and medallions set around and between the different scenes. While the *ko-sometsuke* wares are, as a rule, typically Chinese in feeling, the Shonzui wares, confined entirely to blue and white, show strong Japanese influence. They are almost unknown outside Japan and they are even unrecognised in the west as Chinese except by a few specia-

---

[1] See Soame Jenyns, 'The Chinese *ko-sometsuke* and Shonzui wares', *Transactions of the Oriental Ceramic Society*, Vol. 34, 1962–63, pp. 13–50, for the first comprehensive account of these wares in a western language.

[2] Attributed to Toytori Tanaka. See Soame Jenyns, *loc. cit.*, p. 16.

lists. They would be passed on one side by the usual collector of the contemporary western transition wares. Perhaps the finest of all the Shonzui wares are the globular jars with flat covers such as that illustrated in Colour Plates H and J. This jar is decorated with three panels, the first with a cock, hen and chickens in a garden (Colour Plate H), the second with a river landscape and the third with a group of precious things. The cover is decorated both outside and inside, on the outside with small circular panels of brocade pattern (*Maramon*), as shown in Colour Plate J(*a*) and on the inside with a large flower whorl surrounded by a complex scroll border (Colour Plate J(*b*)). On the base is the inscription 'Made by Gorodaiyu wu Shonzui'. A good deal has been written in Japan about the identification of Shonzui. According to one tradition he was a Japanese potter who went to China to learn Chinese methods in the early sixteenth century. But there are many other traditions which are given various degrees of credence. These can have little relation to the Shonzui wares as we know them, which were made long after the date at which Shonzui is supposed to have lived.

The 'western transition wares' were first made in the T'ien-ch'i period. Thus they must have overlapped both the *ko-sometsuke* and the Shonzui wares. As Japanese and western collectors have been working, so to speak, in watertight compartments, it does not seem to have occurred to anyone to enquire how the eastern and western transition wares are related, if at all, to each other. But even a casual comparison of the western transition wares with the Shonzui wares suggests that, as far as their technical qualities are concerned they have much in common. The aesthetic approach is different in the two types, but nevertheless we can detect at times certain similarities in the treatment of landscapes. It would not be surprising if the two groups were made in closely associated kilns.

The *ko-sometsuke* wares, on the other hand, are very different in their technical qualities from the other two types. There can be little doubt that all the western transition and Shonzui wares were made at Ching-tê Chên, but one is tempted to think that some of the *ko-sometsuke* wares were made in a different district. Jenyns has suggested that a minority of them may have been made in the province of Fukien,[1] but Kikutaro Saito, the great Japanese authority on the *ko-sometsuke* wares, believes that they were all made in private kilns in Ching-tê Chên.[2]

The salient qualities of the three types of transition ware may be studied in the four new colour slides that have been added to this

[1] Jenyns, *loc. cit.*, pp. 13, 17.　　　　　　　　[2] Jenyns, *loc. cit.*, p. 14.

volume. (Colour Plates F to J.) Colour Plate F shows a typical western transition vase, Colour Plate G a *ko-sometsuke* dish of the T'ien-ch'i period and Plates H and J illustrate one of the most important of the Shonzui jars. The two illustrations of Plate J show the outside and inside of the cover.

I cannot do better, in leaving the complex and intriguing question of the inter-relation of the seventeenth-century types, than quote from a letter written by Kikutaro Saito to Soame Jenyns in which he says 'I would like you to get away from the old Shonzui fairy stories and see the Shonzui problem from the point of view of ceramic history; to make active use of the raw materials for the study of Ch'ung-chêng *sometsuke* and to discuss Shonzui from this angle.'[1] This realistic approach might well be extended to cover the *ko-sometsuke* and western transition wares as well. But, as Jenyns has pointed out, the Shonzui fairy stories are liable to prove more fascinating to the art historian than the more mundane studies proposed by Saito. Perhaps east and west could combine in the study of this important ceramic problem. What seems to be needed, more than anything else, is a study of the records of the Ching-tê Chên factories during the late Ming and Ch'ing dynasties, together with the contemporary Japanese records.

As in the text of the second edition, I have resisted the temptation to revise the text of this edition in any way. This preface has dealt with what seem to me to be the most important new points that have arisen. The six new colour plates include four whose main function is to throw light on the new knowledge that has been gained on the seventeenth-century transition wares. The other two illustrate a fine early fourteenth-century pear-shaped vase with figures in a landscape (Colour Plate A), and a beautiful small jar of the Ch'êng-hua period (Colour Plate C), both from Japanese private collections. In the fields of Japanese and Korean blue and white, the appearance during the last few years of new books covering the ceramic art of these two countries by Soame Jenyns[2] and G. St. G. M. Gompertz[3] respectively adds much to our knowledge of the blue and white wares. They should be consulted by those who wish to gain more information than can be given in the restricted scope of this book.

A few references to important works published in the last ten years have been added to the bibliography at the end of the book.

H.M.G.

[1] Jenyns, *loc. cit.*, p. 48.
[2] Soame Jenyns, *Japanese Porcelain*, London, 1965.
[3] G. St. G. M. Gompertz, *Korean Pottery and Porcelain of the Yi Period*, London, 1968.

PREFACE TO THE SECOND EDITION

In the ten years that have elapsed since *Oriental blue and white* was written a great deal of work has been done which calls for some reappraisal of the subject. But on the whole the pattern of development of blue and white, from its first appearance down to the nineteenth century, remains substantially as it was depicted ten years ago.

In some ways, the timing of the publication of *Oriental blue and white* was fortunate. Our knowledge of the early Chinese blue and white wares was very sketchy before 1930, as a glance at Hobson's *Wares of the Ming dynasty*, a book well in the van of western knowledge when published in 1923, will show. The education of the western world in the classical fifteenth century types, which of course were fully understood by connoisseurs in China, came through the influence of western visitors to China, such as Sir Percival David and A. D. Brankston. By the early 1930's serious western students were beginning to become familiar with fifteenth century blue and white. But the fourteenth century wares, made mainly for export to the near east, were as yet almost unrecognised, although there were a number of pieces in western collections. Unrepresented in the Chinese imperial collection and apparently unknown among connoisseurs in China, fourteenth century blue and white has been identified and classified entirely by the efforts of western scholars. However, the touchstone that sparked off the train of events which finally led to the identification was provided by the well known vases, datable to 1351, now in the Percival David Foundation, which came from China in 1928. It was natural that these complex and imposing pieces should be viewed with some reservation at first but gradually their close resemblance to some of the pieces in the Sarayi Museum at Istanbul, known to have been in the west since Ming times, became evident. The comparison had the two-fold effect of establishing the authenticity of the David vases and dating the Istanbul pieces as belonging to the fourteenth century. The illustrations of one of the David vases (Plate 6) and a vase at Istanbul (Plate 7) shows the close connection which finally led to the firm identification of fourteenth century blue and white.

The thorough and detailed studies by John Pope of the wares at Istanbul and the still more important collection, formerly at Ardebil and now at Teheran, enabled fourteenth century blue and white to be fitted into an orderly arrangement. *Oriental blue and white* was written before his studies of the Ardebil Collection were complete, and it suffered a little in consequence—not a single piece from Ardebil is illustrated in the book—but knowledge of the fourteenth century wares was sufficiently advanced for a sound survey to be made. A few years earlier this would not have been possible.

Since then more work has been done on the early blue and white wares and the associated wares decorated in copper red, as well as the white wares of the early Yüan period, particularly by Arthur Lane and John Ayers.[1] This period was one of intensive experimentation in which numerous techniques in moulding, carving and the application of slip, as well as painting in cobalt, copper and iron, and the use of glazes in these materials, were attempted. By the fifteenth century painting in cobalt blue had emerged as the most successful and popular technique, and it remained so throughout the whole of the Ming dynasty. Painting in copper red was so uncertain in its results that it was reserved for special types. Nevertheless in the early stages, the study of blue and white should be closely allied with that of painting in copper red.

These more recent studies suggest that the period of experimentation started round about 1300 and the view, expressed in *Oriental blue and white*, that the first pieces of blue and white were made round about the turn of the fourteenth century, does not seem to have been shaken. There is no evidence to support the view, which is advanced from time to time, that blue and white wares were made in the Sung dynasty.

One of the most important developments since *Oriental blue and white* was written is the attempt that has been made to distinguish between the wares made in the different parts of the fifteenth century and particularly to sort out those of the so-called 'inter-regnum period', which stretched from the end of the reign of Hsüan-tê (1435) to the accession of Ch'êng-hua (1465). Even ten years ago I expressed the view that many pieces, either bearing the Hsüan-tê mark or ascribed to the period, may have been made during the inter-regnum period (see pp. 24–25) and since then further doubts about some of these pieces have been expressed by others. The pieces illustrated in Plates 23, 26A, 27C and 30B, to mention a few, may well belong to the second rather than the first half of the century. They include some of the most attractive fifteenth century wares.

[1] John Ayers. *Some characteristic wares of the Yüan dynasty*. Oriental Ceramic Society Transactions, 1954–55.

PREFACE TO THE SECOND EDITION

These tentative views on the attribution of blue and white wares to the inter-regnum period, based on general observation and studies of stylistic detail, were not likely to convince the sceptics who have inherited the Chinese tradition of the sanctity of imperial fifteenth century wares bearing the Hsüan-tê mark. But recently an attempt to distinguish between the types belonging to the different periods of the fifteenth century, made by Margaret Medley, working mainly on material in the Percival David Foundation, has met with remarkable success.[1, 2] Definite distinguishing characteristics in the glazes of pieces in different groups have been found and there can be no doubt that this study, still in its early stages, will lead to a much better knowledge of the dates of manufacture of fifteenth century wares. But it will be some time before an orderly arrangement is established. Moreover, we cannot be entirely satisfied with any conclusions reached until we can understand the changing conditions of manufacture during the fifteenth century that led to the differences in glaze structure.

As compared with the fifteenth century, the sixteenth presents little difficulty and there is not much that could be added. The seventeenth century, covering the decline of the Ming dynasty and the rise of the Ch'ing, one of the most interesting and stimulating periods in the history of the decorative arts of China, presents some fascinating problems and the brief treatment given in *Oriental blue and white* cannot claim to be entirely adequate. The standard so-called 'transitional wares', so well represented in European country houses, have long been understood, if not, until recently, appreciated as they deserve. These are briefly but adequately dealt with. But the more roughly made wares of a slightly earlier period, often bearing the T'ien-ch'i mark, and the so-called Shonzui wares belonging to the Ch'ung-chêng reign, made for the Japanese market and highly appreciated in Japan today, are hardly to be found in the west and we have to go to Japan for information about them. The recent studies of these wares by Soame Jenyns[3] sum up the latest information from Japan and should be incorporated in any book claiming to deal authoritatively with seventeenth century blue and white.

In the history of the development of blue and white porcelain there were periods, such as the fourteenth and the middle of the seventeenth

[1] Margaret Medley, *Illustrated catalogue of porcelain decorated in underglaze blue and copper red in the Percival David Foundation of Chinese art*, 1963.

[2] Margaret Medley, *Regrouping fifteenth century blue and white*, Oriental Ceramic Society Transactions, 1963–64.

[3] Soame Jenyns, *The Chinese Ko-Sometsuke and Shonzui wares*, Oriental Ceramic Society Transactions, 1963–64.

centuries when the demand was mainly from outside China. But even in the fifteenth and sixteenth centuries, when the imperial demand was enormous, a great deal of blue and white was exported to Indonesia, the Philippines and Malaya, and many places further afield, as we know from the evidence of excavations. Some of the excavated pieces are similar to the imperial wares, although of coarser quality, but there are others which we cannot, at present, connect with any Chinese wares known to us. One of the most interesting groups is that illustrated in Plates 84, 85 and 86A, which has been ascribed to Annam. They are very distinctive wares and appear to go back to the early fifteenth century, if not earlier. The attribution to Annam is no better established now than it was ten years ago and it is possible that these wares were made in Southern China rather than Indo-China. They may have no more connection with Annam than the so-called 'Swatow wares' have with Swatow. Now that excavations in China are being made under careful control we may expect more information about blue and white kiln sites, and the connection between the local and export wares to be more closely established.

The emphasis in the study of blue and white porcelain during the next ten years or so may be expected to be concentrated in two main directions, the closer dating of the fifteenth century wares and the identification of the places of manufacture of the so-called 'provincial wares'. Most of the fine porcelain for the court and the wealthy classes in the Ming and Ch'ing dynasties was made at Ching-tê Chên, and a good deal of inferior porcelain was made there also. But there can be no doubt that there were many places in South China outside Ching-tê Chên where blue and white was made and the identification of these kiln sites will enable us to get a much clearer picture of the vast production of the export wares than we have at present. This in turn will enable us to see the imperial wares in a truer perspective. The tendency of most collectors to concentrate on pieces of the finest quality gives a distorted picture of blue and white in the Ming dynasty and a closer study of the less sophisticated, but often more lively export wares will provide a much needed corrective.

The text of the first edition remains substantially unaltered and the temptation to introduce emendations here and there has been resisted. The book must stand in the light of knowledge at the time of publication. Correction of obvious mistakes, fortunately not extensive, have been made and parts of pp. 2 and 3 which seemed to be misleading have been rewritten.

H.M.G.

1

INTRODUCTION

In the long history of the development of decorated pottery and porcelain, no single type has had a more widespread influence than that which is now known as blue and white. It reached its heyday in China during the Ming dynasty and its manufacture spread to the countries of the Near East, to the other oriental countries Japan and Korea, and finally to Europe. Although from the early eighteenth century onwards the more brightly coloured porcelains came into favour everywhere, blue and white still retained much of its popularity. In England, for example, the printed wares of Staffordshire were largely blue and white and in many instances, such as the well-known Willow Pattern, were based on Chinese designs.

Although the story of the development of blue and white is generally associated with China, it was not there, but in the Near East, that the method of painting designs in cobalt oxide to produce a blue colour was first developed. In the ninth century a type of rather soft pottery was produced in Mesopotamia which, after being covered with an opaque white glaze containing tin oxide to conceal the coloured body, was painted with simple designs in cobalt oxide and then fired. This technique of painting is similar to that adopted later in Italian maiolica and Dutch and English delftware.

In China itself the painting of pottery with a blue glaze containing cobalt was actually developed towards the end of the T'ang dynasty. Blue was used either as a single glaze, or in combination with yellow-brown, green and white. The glazes were sometimes applied in splashed decoration and sometimes to fill in designs incised or stamped out on the pottery. These designs have a close resemblance to those on silver dishes[1] made in eastern Europe or western Asia during the early centuries of our era. It is a long way from these designs and from the techniques adopted to those of the early blue and white porcelains and it seems unlikely that the T'ang blue glazes had much influence on the later wares.

The blue painting just described, both Near-Eastern and Chinese,

[1] H. C. Gallois, *About T'ang and Ta Ts'in*, O.C.S. Trans. 1935–36.

was not covered with a glaze. The method of painting in blue under a transparent glaze was first used by the Persian potters at Kashan in the thirteenth century.[1] The blue pigment was applied directly to the body, a hard semi-translucent pottery somewhat similar to the later European soft paste porcelain. This pottery was evidently made in imitation of one of the Chinese Sung types, either Ting or *ying ch'ing*, both of which were imported into the Near East and greatly admired there. The blue pigment, although good in colour, was not satisfactory, because it ran badly, and its use seems to have been restricted to broad bands of decoration, or to filling in outlines made in a black pigment which was more tractable.

The method of manufacture of the early Chinese blue and white did not differ very much, in essentials, from that of the Persian. The Chinese tried a number of techniques in the early days, sometimes covering the body with a slip or opaque glaze and sometimes painting directly on to it. The piece was then usually covered with a transparent glaze and fired at a high temperature, but there is reason to think that such a glaze was not always used in the early pieces. The important difference between the Chinese and the Persian wares is not in these details of technique but in the material of the body. The Chinese used a true felspathic porcelain and covered it with a felspathic glaze which united with the body in firing to a remarkable degree. They were also able, at an early stage in the development of blue and white, to control the blue pigment so that designs could be painted in great detail.

Although the exact date at which the Chinese first made blue and white cannot yet be ascertained, the evidence that we have at present suggests that manufacture was not started much before the beginning of the fourteenth century. The question naturally arises as to the extent to which the Chinese were influenced in their early blue and white by the Persian wares. There was a good deal of intercourse between eastern and western Asia in the thirteenth and fourteenth centuries, during the Mongolian Yüan dynasty, and there is evidence to support the view that the Chinese were well acquainted with the Near-Eastern wares. But the Chinese designs bear little relation to the Near-Eastern ones and it is probable that the Chinese potters learned little more than that an attractive colour could be obtained by the use of cobalt, applied under a trans-lucent felspathic glaze.

As we have seen, the Chinese were acquainted with the use of cobalt as early as the T'ang dynasty. Such scanty evidence as we have about

---

[1] Lane, *Early Islamic Pottery*, p. 45.

the T'ang blue glazes suggests that the cobalt was imported from Persia.[1]

The view that early Chinese blue and white owed little to outside influence is supported by the fact that the Chinese, in the days of early development, were painting porcelain in red designs similar to those in blue. The technique of painting in copper oxide and firing in a reducing atmosphere to give a red colour was purely Chinese. The designs seem to have been generally, if not always, applied under the glaze, in contrast to the later pieces of the Ch'ing dynasty, in which the designs were applied invariably over the glaze, and so conformed to the usual practice adopted in cobalt painting.[2] The existence of similar designs in blue and red on primitive porcelains suggests that the Chinese potters were experimenting in order to obtain a good and reliable colour. The conditions necessary to give a good red colour from copper oxide are critical and we find that in most of the Chinese early red and white pieces the colour is a dull brown or grey, although occasionally a piece of good colour is seen. It is clear that the method was unreliable and we find that the use of copper oxide after the fourteenth century was retained only for the manufacture of a few special classes of porcelain. It was not until the seventeenth century that the technique of painting in copper red was thoroughly mastered. Blue and white, on the other hand, proved much more tractable, and it was not long before the Chinese potters had obtained complete mastery of the technique of its manufacture.

*　　*　　*　　*　　*　　*　　*

Oriental blue and white, particularly that made in China, has had during the whole period of its development a unique quality which has never been approached in any other blue and white porcelain. The reasons for this can be appreciated if the method of manufacture is studied in detail. We know a good deal about the Chinese methods from letters sent by Père d'Entrecolles, a Jesuit missionary who lived in Ching-tê Chên, in the southern province of Kiangsi, the main centre of manufacture of blue and white in China, in the early eighteenth century.[3] The information given in these letters has been

[1] See the analyses made by W. J. Young, *Far-Eastern Ceramic Bulletin*, 1949.

[2] The view that cobalt designs were sometimes applied over the glaze has been put forward by some modern potters, and Mr. Roger Bluett has pointed out that some fragments of early blue and white show the blue colour entirely over the glaze.

[3] The letters are reproduced in full in an Appendix to Bushell's *Description of Chinese Pottery and Porcelain*, (*being a translation of the T'ao Shuo*), 1910.

supplemented from other sources and checked by examination and analysis of specimens, so that we have reliable information on how the porcelain was actually made. Two materials, in the main, were used, china-clay and china-stone. China-stone is a feldspar, either potassium or sodium. It is a crystalline substance which is found naturally, sometimes in igneous rocks such as granite and sometimes in an almost pure form. China-clay, which has been produced by the natural decay of feldspar, during which the potassium or sodium has been lost, is a hydrated silicate of aluminium.

Both these materials are found in large quantities near Ching-tê Chên. The Chinese called the china-clay *kaolin*, meaning 'high ridge', from the place where it was found, and the china-stone *pai-tun-tzu* meaning 'little white bricks', a reference to the small bricks into which the pulverised substance was moulded. Although both materials contained impurities which had to be removed, there is no doubt that they were of very high quality and the growth of Ching-tê Chên to become the most important centre of manufacture in China was due to its fortunate situation near to plentiful supplies of high-grade raw materials.

The china-clay has plastic qualities which enable it to be easily moulded, while china-stone is fusible and in the fused state is transparent. The two materials can be combined readily and a mixture is used to make the body of the porcelain. When they are mixed in the right proportion and fired at the right temperature (about 1350° C.) a white semi-opaque porcelain is produced. Père d'Entrecolles tells us that the Chinese describe china-clay and china-stone as the 'bones' and the 'flesh'. This, although not scientific, is a good description that enables the non-expert student to get an idea of the functions of the two materials. The glaze is made from china-stone with the addition of a little lime and wood ash to help in the fusing.

Chinese blue and white is fired once only. The body is allowed to dry, the pigment is applied to the unglazed body, the whole is covered with glaze and the piece is fired.[1] Because of the kinship of the materials used for the glaze and the paste, the fusion is complete. If a section of the fired ware is examined the original junction of the body and glaze is barely discernible. The blue colour is suspended between the outer surface and the body in a glaze which is sufficiently transparent to enable the colour to be clearly seen, while the increase

[1] Early exceptions to this method have been referred to. The practice of covering the body with a slip in order to give a whiter and smoother surface seems to have been practised in the fourteenth century and may possibly, on occasions, have been used later. Brankston points out in his *Early Ming Wares of Ching-tê Chên* that in China today a weak slip is used to detect flaws and produce a smooth surface.

4

B. HSÜAN TÊ MARK AND PERIOD. HT. 14.0 in.
See page 22

in opacity towards the body removes all harshness from the background. The result, in the best blue and white, is a brilliance and luminosity unequalled in the field of ceramics.

There is a great variety in the colour of the blue and, no less important, of the white glaze which is generally greenish or bluish. Particular shades were popular in different periods and we shall discuss these later. The colour of the blue depends on the purity of the cobalt and its concentration in the glaze. If the cobalt is free from impurities, particularly iron and manganese, and is not too concentrated, a pure blue colour is obtained. When the cobalt is concentrated the colour becomes blackish and, in heavier concentrations still, red-black. Rusty spots showing excessive concentration are occasionally found in all periods but are particularly evident in the 'heaped and piled' decoration of the earlier wares. When the concentration of cobalt is low, as happens when a thick glaze is applied, the colour is pale and diffuse. When iron and manganese, the usual impurities, are present the colour becomes greyish.

The greenish or bluish tint in the white is caused by iron impurities in the glaze and is the result of the piece being fired in a reducing atmosphere. In an oxidising atmosphere the colour would be a pale buff, and one type of eighteenth century blue and white, generally known as 'soft paste', appears to be an exception in that it was generally fired in this way. It has often been stated that a reducing atmosphere is necessary to produce a pure colour in the blue decoration but there is no evidence that the colour is materially affected by the amount of oxidation that occurs. Certainly modern European blue and white is generally fired in an oxidising atmosphere.

The Chinese do not seem to have had a native source of cobalt free from manganese, and this accounts for the great importance attached to the imported 'Mohammedan blue'. But without doubt empirical methods were developed throughout the Ming dynasty for separating the impurities from the cobalt and these methods were capable, by the end of the dynasty, of producing cobalt sufficiently pure to give an excellent colour. The method used in the nineteenth century is described by T. I. Bowler, who saw it in use.[1] He was greatly surprised to find that 'these ingenious and very peculiar people' were able by simple methods to remove iron, nickel and manganese from the crude ore.'

Père d'Entrecolles' description of the making of blue and white is admirable. 'A beautiful blue colour appears on porcelain after having been lost for some time. When the colour is first painted on, it is pale black; when it is dry and the glaze has been put on it, it disappears

[1] *Chemical News*, August 31st, 1888.

entirely and the porcelain seems quite white, the colour being buried under the glaze. But the fire makes it appear in all its beauty, almost in the same way as the natural heat of the sun makes the most beautiful butterflies, with all their tints, come out of their eggs.'

* * * * * * *

The dating of oriental blue and white, covering something like six hundred years in China and three hundred in Korea and Japan, presents some fascinating problems. While the greater part of the porcelain can easily be placed in identified groups there is a small part for which the date of manufacture, and sometimes even the country of origin cannot be easily determined. Porcelain was regarded as of great artistic value and the earlier wares, as they became rare, were copied. Some of the copies were very good and a careful study of the method of manufacture, the material of the body and glaze, the colour of the blue and the style of the drawing, including that of the mark, is necessary before a reliable judgment can be formed.

In the earlier periods of pottery and porcelain manufacture some evidence is available from the excavation of tomb and kiln sites. The practice of burial of pottery and porcelain in tombs, however, had begun to die out by the time that blue and white porcelain was being made and the amount of evidence from tombs is small. Few systematic excavations of kiln sites have been made and more are badly needed.

In the later periods more reliable evidence on the dating of blue and white can be obtained at the present time from Western and Near-Eastern sources rather than from Far-Eastern.[1] The porcelain was exported in increasing quantities from the fourteenth century onwards, first to the Near East and then to Europe. One of the most valuable sources of evidence is provided by the large collection formed by Shah Abbas the Great which he presented in 1611 to the shrine of Shaikh Safi at Ardebil. The pieces were incised with his seal and we can be reasonably certain that the remnant of the collection, now at Teheran, consists of pieces made before 1611. Another fine collection of early blue and white is in the Serai at Istanbul.

The blue and white imported into Europe was held in very high esteem and is frequently described in detail in old inventories. Some of the pieces were fitted with silver mounts which are sometimes dated and thus provide some information on the date of manufacture of the porcelain itself. In the eighteenth century many pieces were made to special European order and some are decorated with armorial

[1] It is possible that when the old Chinese records can be fully studied much further information will be revealed. At present many of these records are not available for study in the West.

bearings which celebrate marriages and therefore can be accurately dated.

Unfortunately the information from Near-Eastern and European sources becomes meagre when we go further back than the middle of the sixteenth century and we have to rely more and more on internal evidence, supported by references to the Chinese literature. These are generally vague and contradictory and must be treated with caution. There are a few pieces which bear inscriptions giving the date of manufacture and these provide valuable supporting evidence.

* * * * * * *

There has been a natural tendency, in recent years, for attention to be concentrated on the early blue and white made in the fourteenth and fifteenth centuries. Previously little known, these pieces with their bold decoration and fine shapes have aroused intense admiration. But the merits of the later Ming and Ch'ing wares must not be overlooked. Fine pieces with high artistic qualities were made in all periods and it was not until the nineteenth century, when the quality of the porcelain itself became poor, that good blue and white was no longer made. The blue and white of the Chia Ching period, with designs in dark purplish blue, the later Ming wares in silvery blue and the K'ang Hsi wares in a pure blue whose technical perfection has never been surpassed, all include pieces of great beauty.

Nor must it be imagined that high qualities were confined to Imperial wares, made for the use of the court. We often find that pieces made for other uses have a vigour and beauty of design which is absent from some of the Imperial wares. In the first half of the seventeenth century, for example, a beautiful class of blue and white known as 'Transition Ware' was made in China. The quality of the best of these pieces, which are generally unmarked, is very high. The marked pieces of this period which bear the mark of T'ien Ch'i or Ch'ung Chêng are generally inferior in quality and colour.

In fact the distinction between Imperial and non-Imperial wares can often not be clearly made. Certain types of decoration, and in particular certain types of dragon and phoenix, were at one time supposed to be confined to Imperial wares. The dragon in Chinese mythology is the lord of the skies and the beneficent bringer of rain. When depicted with five claws on each foot he is the symbol of the Emperor[1] and porcelain made for Imperial use is often decorated with five-clawed dragons. Dragons with four or three claws are supposed to be symbolic of a descending social status. But we know from the

[1] In the T'ang and Sung dynasties all the dragons were three-clawed. See S. Cammann, *China's Dragon Robes.*

7

evidence of dated pieces that, at any rate from the early sixteenth century onwards, pieces decorated with five-clawed dragons were made for members of the Emperor's household and others. There is for example an incense burner in three coloured enamel decoration in the Museum of Fine Arts, Boston, which bears an inscription showing that it was made in the Chêng Tê period for the head of the Emperor's cavalry.[1] A blue and white jar of the Wan Li period with similar dragons (1) was made for presentation by the donor, whose social status is not revealed, to a temple in Shansi. Conversely marked pieces of Imperial quality, such as the Mayer bowl[2] are sometimes decorated with dragons with three claws. Thus it seems desirable not to place too much reliance on Imperial attributions but to judge pieces by their artistic and technical qualities.

Although the main centre of manufacture of blue and white in China was confined to a small area of Kiangsi in the neighbourhood of Ching-tê Chên, blue and white was made in many other provinces in China. We have evidence from a dated piece that blue and white of good quality was made in the province of Annam, in Indo-China, in the mid-fifteenth century (2) and an extensive group of blue and white pieces found in the Philippine Islands is attributed to Annam. A distinct type of blue and white was also made in the province of Fukien as early as the seventeenth century, or possibly even earlier. This porcelain seems to have had a great influence on the manifacture of blue and white in Japan.

The Japanese and Korean blue and white cover a shorter period of development and a more limited range of types than the Chinese. The Japanese blue and white familiar to Western collectors is generally of the type made for export and the special porcelain made for the wealthy princes is hardly known outside Japan. The reputation of Korea lies mainly in its fine early celadon wares but the blue and white, developed at a late stage in Korean ceramic history, has great merit. The wares are primitive, but although the colour of the blue is greyish and the general finish crude, they have a vigour and beauty which makes them more attractive than some of the more highly sophisticated wares.

[1] See Jenyns, *Pottery and Porcelain of the Ming Dynasty*, Plate 83A.
[2] Detroit Exhibition, *Arts of the Ming Dynasty*, 1952, No. 100.

(1) *Plate* 54; (2) *Plate* 84A.

2

ORIGIN OF BLUE AND WHITE

We may reasonably infer that the early Chinese blue and white porcelain was developed from one of the white Sung porcelains. The most likely of these is that known as *ying ch'ing* and the view most strongly supported today is that blue and white was developed from the *shu-fu* porcelain of the Yüan dynasty which was itself developed from *ying ch'ing*.

Ying ch'ing (shadow blue) is a thin translucent white porcelain covered with a clear glaze of bluish tint. The term is a modern one, invented by Chinese dealers, which has unfortunately become established in the West. The identity of this ware with any of those referred to in the Chinese literature has not yet been determined. Sir Percival David has suggested that the term *ch'ing pai* (greenish or bluish white), which is used in the official report of the Imperial connoisseur Chiang Ch'i, the *Tao chi luo*, first published in 1325 and subsequently widely reprinted in the *Fou liang hsien chih*[1] and other books, should be used in describing these wares.

Fragments of *ying ch'ing* found at Fostat were analysed by Sir Herbert Jackson and found to consist of a soft porcelain fired at a temperature of about 900° C.[2] Some of the *ying ch'ing* wares are, however, much harder than this and must have been fired at a higher temperature. *Ying ch'ing* was made over a wide area in China and it is not surprising that there are large variations in body and glaze, and in the technique of manufacture. A large number of *ying ch'ing* fragments have been excavated in China, particularly near Ching-tê Chên.

Shu-fu (privy council)[3] ware is referred to in the *Ko-ku Yao-lun*, printed in 1387. It is stated to have been made in the Yüan dynasty and is the earliest known ware made at Ching-tê Chên to official orders. It is porcelain covered with a bluish-white glaze and usually consists of bowls and dishes with a moulded or slip decoration inside,

[1] See Bushell, *Oriental Ceramic Art*, p. 179, where the term *ch'ing pai* is wrongly translated as 'celadon'.
[2] O.C.S. Trans. 1926–27.
[3] Or 'central palace'.

often in the form of flower sprays. The decoration sometimes includes the characters *shu-fu*, indicating the official use of the piece. The characters are concealed in the decoration and are sometimes difficult to find. Some dishes are known with good wish characters such as *fu* (happiness), *lu* (emolument) and *shou* (longevity).

Large quantities of fragments, including wasters, of *ying ch'ing* and blue and white were found by Brankston[1] at Hu-t'ien, near Ching-tê Chên. *Ying ch'ing* and *shu-fu* fragments have also been found at Nan-Shan, a few miles away. There is a strong presumption from the evidence that blue and white was developed from *ying ch'ing* and *shu-fu*.

There are a number of blue and white bowls that resemble closely *shu-fu* pieces both in the material of the body and glaze and in the method of construction.[2] These pieces are often decorated in a free style, with simple sprays of leaves and flowers of daisies or lotus, often ending in a group of buds or berries. Two jars with this type of decoration are shown in Plates 1A, 1B. They may well be among the earliest pieces of blue and white known and probably belong to the beginning of the fourteenth century. Jars similar to the second of these jars, with covers in the shape of a lotus leaf, are known in celadon. They are generally attributed to the Yüan dynasty. A third jar (1), with a rather more advanced style of decoration, may be a little later than the other two. It has a cover with a deep ridge inside to which there are close parallels also in celadons attributed to the Yüan dynasty.

Also belonging to the earliest period of blue and white are the stem cups which bear, in addition to dragons in blue on the outside of the bowl (2), dragons or flower scrolls in slip or moulded decoration on the inside. Stem cups with the moulded dragon design and without any blue decoration are known. The body and glaze of these pieces and the moulded and slip decoration resemble closely those of the marked *shu-fu* pieces. One of the blue and white stem cups, in the Victoria and Albert Museum, has been found to have the character *yü* (jade) in the moulded decoration, which provides a further link with *shu-fu*. One dragon stem cup in the Museum of Asiatic Art, Oxford, rather smaller than the rest, has blue dragons outside and the eight precious emblems inside in slip decoration. *Shu-fu* bowls with this decoration are known and we shall see later that these emblems are found in blue and white on the David vases dated 1351 and other pieces.

[1] *O.C.S. Trans.*, 1938–39, pp. 19–32.
[2] Kamer Aga-Oglu, *Far Eastern Ceramic Bulletin*, December 1949.

(1) *Plate* 1C; (2) *Plate* 2A.

Another stem cup (1), decorated in slip with flower scrolls inside, has a very simple design in blackish brown outside and in the centre of the bowl, in what seems to be an attempt at painting in cobalt blue which has gone wrong in the firing. The contrast between the elementary painted decoration and the slip decoration inside, which has great refinement, suggests that this may be one of the earliest experiments in blue and white, applied to a well established *shu-fu* type.

A curious feature of the dragon stem cups is that the blue dragons are three-clawed while the moulded dragons are four-clawed. We have already pointed out that too much significance must not be attached to the number of claws and this early example of inconsistency supports the argument. A dish in the Clark collection (2) with three clouds in the centre, has moulded five-clawed dragons surrounding the clouds and blue five-clawed dragons underneath. This may be a little later than the stem cups, but it has every indication of being an early piece, and furthermore an early example of the use of five-clawed dragons on a piece not of Imperial quality. This dish provides a link with the later Imperial dishes bearing the Hsüan Tê mark. These also have dragons in slip inside[1] and in blue outside.

Other early pieces of blue and white are a number of pear-shaped bottles, one of which is decorated with a dragon similar to those on the stem cups (3). Another type is decorated with flowing scrolls of chrysanthemums. One of these (4), now in the British Museum,[2] was stated to have come from a Sung tomb, but the evidence for this is not convincing. These pear-shaped bottles are known with other designs in blue and white[3] and there are also some primitive ones with simple decoration in copper red.[4]

There are also vases of baluster form with side handles and horizontal bands of decoration (5). A feature of these vases is the hollow unglazed base, which is often two or three inches deep. A number of clever forgeries of this type were made some years ago, in which the effects of burial have been simulated. They can be distinguished by their stiff drawing.

A brief reference has been made to the two vases in the David Foundation, dated 1351. These vases are the only fully documented pieces of blue and white of the fourteenth century at present known to us (6). They are tall and slender, fitted with elephant-head side

[1] But in a fine *an hua* (hidden) style, very different from the bold style of the earlier dish.
[2] There is another in the Art Institute of Chicago.
[3] *Philadelphia Museum Bulletin*, No. 223, Nos. 2, 3.
[4] See Jenyns, *Ming Pottery and Porcelain*, Plate 6B.

(1) *Plate* 2B; (2) Plate 2C; (3) Plate 3; (4) Plate 4; (5) *Plate* 5; (6) *Plate* 6.

handles that originally supported rings. The decoration is in horizontal bands, the main subject being a four-clawed dragon in clouds and above waves. The other subjects of decoration include phoenixes in clouds, scrolling paeonies, waves in bold serpentine form and a collection of emblems. We have noted that the last appear in slip on an early dragon stem cup. Each vase bears a long inscription on the neck dated 1351 stating that the vases, together with an incense burner, were presented by Chang Wên-chin to a temple of Hu-Ching-i, one of the minor deities. The home of the donor has been identified, from the inscription, as a town seventy miles from Ching-tê Chên.

The David vases are more complex in construction and decoration than the simple pieces that have already been described and it is convenient to regard them as marking the end of the early development of blue and white although there were, of course, no real lines of demarcation. At one time students of Chinese ceramics were reluctant to accept the David vases as being so early as the mid-fourteenth century because they seemed to stand alone in their complexity of design and decoration. We shall see later that recent studies of the great collections at Istanbul and Teheran, as well as of many pieces in Western collections, have produced a number of parallel pieces, and the David vases are now clearly established as providing the most important landmark in the early history of blue and white.

We have already referred to the early experiments of the Chinese potters with a copper pigment to give designs in red. Although outside the scope of this book, these wares are of great interest because it would seem that the decision to develop blue and white and abandon almost entirely red and white was made when the difficulty of getting a good colour was found to be almost insurmountable.

The earliest pieces of blue and white were painted in a blackish blue, often discoloured with rusty spots, and generally covered with a thick bluish glaze. Most if not all of them are excavated wares and have acquired a dull surface as the result of burial. The blue of the David vases is finer, one of the vases in particular being painted in a brilliant purplish blue.

Blue and white in the first half of the fourteenth century was still in its early development and had not yet reached the stage of being accorded Imperial favour. No doubt monochromes of the types developed in the Sung dynasty were preferred. But before the end of the century dishes, vases and jars of fine quality were being made in blue and white, destined to lead to the highest achievements of the fifteenth century.

12

C. CH'ÊNG-HUA MARK AND PERIOD. HT. 4.3 in.
Japanese Collection
See page xxvi

3

THE LATE FOURTEENTH AND EARLY FIFTEENTH CENTURIES

By the time of manufacture of the David vases, and possibly some time before then, blue and white had reached a stage at which mastery of the medium had been attained and definite styles of painting established. There are no further landmarks, similar to these vases, until we reach the pieces marked with the reign mark (*nien hao*) of Hsüan Tê (1426–1435). During the seventy-four years that elapsed between the making of the vases and the ascent to the throne of Hsüan Tê there were considerable changes in design and technique. But we have no means yet of indicating when these changes took place and we must rely, for dating purposes, on internal evidence and conjecture. There is no evidence that any violent changes took place during this period, and it seems likely that the changes from what we may call typical fourteenth to typical fifteenth century styles took place gradually. It is therefore convenient to treat this period of seventy-four years as a whole, and as a period of development leading to the classical reigns of the fifteenth century.

*   *   *   *   *   *   *

Until about 1920 what we now know to be early blue and white was unrecognised in the Western countries. Although a large number of early dishes and jars with unglazed bases have been in western collections for many years—there is a fifteenth century dish actually with the Hsüan Tê mark (1) which has been in the Victoria and Albert Museum since 1870—they were assumed to be either late Ming or Ch'ing pieces. The two greatest collections of early export wares, at Istanbul and Teheran, had not been fully studied. These export or non-Imperial wares, many of which belong to the fourteenth and fifteenth centuries, rarely bear the mark of a Chinese Emperor, but a number of fifteenth-century pieces bearing the marks of Hsüan Tê or other Emperors of the fifteenth century began to

(1) *Plate* 16.

arrive in Western countries about twenty-five years ago. These have been studied and compared with the non-Imperial wares. As a result the pattern of fourteenth and fifteenth century blue and white is becoming clearer. But there are difficult gaps to be filled and much further study is needed before the pattern will be complete.

We are fortunate in the existence of the large collection of blue and white porcelain at Teheran, containing a number of pieces which were presented by Shah Abbas the Great to the shrine of Shaikh Safi at Ardebil and bear his incised seal, known to have been applied at a date before 1611. This rules out the possibility of any of the pieces being late copies, and since the qualities of sixteenth century blue and white differ greatly from those of the fourteenth and fifteenth centuries we are able to ascribe many of the pieces with some confidence to the earlier period. A recent thorough study of the collection by Pope[1] suggests that there are about two hundred such pieces. The collection in the Serai at Istanbul was examined in some detail by Zimmermann in 1930[2] but a further and more comprehensive study by Pope[3] has placed the early wares in a much more accurate perspective.

The quality of the pieces in the Near Eastern collections and the similar pieces that have found their way to the West is very high. Although they are generally described as export wares and are unmarked, the potting and decoration of many of them are not inferior to those of the marked pieces obtained from China during the last thirty years and which, for the most part, have no doubt come from the Imperial collections. The dishes, jars, vases and ewers, although heavily potted as is fitting for vessels intended for regular use, are carefully finished. The bases are almost always unglazed and are generally coloured red-brown, the effect of firing on the iron in the paste, but when the bases have been scoured by abrasion—and many of the dishes have been treated in this way—a fine-grained pure white porcelain is seen.

During the seventy-four years that elapsed between the making of the David vases and the ascent to the throne of Hsüan Tê there were naturally great variations in the style of painting, the quality of the pigments used and the conditions of firing. The colour of the blue is found to vary from a dull greyish blue to an almost pure ultramarine, and some pieces are known painted in a dark purplish blue which approaches that regarded as typical of Chia Ching Imperial pieces. Indeed the colour of the blue may be regarded as the least satisfactory

---

[1] Pope, *Harvard Journal of Asiatic Studies*, December 1950. See also an article by Bahrami, *O.C.S. Trans.*, 1949–50.

[2] Zimmermann, *Altchinesische Porzellan im Alten Serai*.

[3] Pope, *Freer Gallery of Art Occasional Papers*, Vol. 2, No. 1, 1952.

criterion to be applied as a means of dating these early pieces. But there are certain qualities which they nearly all possess. There is a freedom of drawing in which the pattern is built up by applying bold splashes of colour rather than by filling in a carefully drawn outline. Where the colour is applied thickly it develops a blackish tinge which contrasts with the purer colour of the rest. The blackish parts are sunk into the glaze, producing an undulating surface which is often described by the term 'heaped and piled'. Sometimes blackish dots are found, generally on the lower sides of the outlines. The glaze is thick and greenish-blue and the surface is slightly uneven. The texture has been likened to that of orange peel.

The early blue and white, and particularly that of the fifteenth century, was extensively copied in the eighteenth century, when an attempt was even made to imitate the technical defects such as the 'heaped and piled' effect, variations in the colour of the blue and dots on the edges of the outlines.[1] There are indeed a few such copies dating from the time of Wan Li. The copies are rarely good enough to deceive. The true 'heaped and piled' effect is seldom obtained, the dots have clearly been deliberately applied and are not accidental, as in the earlier wares, and there are differences in material and construction. But the later copies can best be distinguished by the drawing, which lacks the vigour and freedom of that of the original.

We know from the Chinese writings that the native sources of cobalt gave an impure blue and there are frequent references to the importation of cobalt ores, variously named *Su-ma-ni*, *Su-ni-p'o* and *hui hui ch'ing* (Mohammedan blue), from the middle east. The *Shi-wu Kan-chu*, printed in 1591, says that imported blue was used in the Yung Lo period, while the Ming Annals state that envoys from Sumatra, bringing *hui hui ch'ing* among other articles of tribute, arrived in China in the years 1426, 1430, 1433 and 1434.

The main source of cobalt in China is asbolite, which contains a large proportion of manganese. This is responsible for a greyish appearance in the blue. A number of Near-Eastern sources of cobalt in the form of arsenates, such as cobaltite and denaite, are known. These ores contain no manganese and would give a purer blue than can be obtained from the Chinese ores.

We are told in later Chinese writings, such as the *T'ang Shi Szu K'ao*,[2] published in 1778, that the Mohammedan blue by itself

---

[1] See Edgar Bluett, 'The Dating of Early Blue and White,' *Oriental Art*, Vol. 1, No. 2. Copies of the Ch'êng Hua period are in a different class and are referred to on p. 26.

[2] For further information on this book, see Sir Percival David, 'A Commentary on Ju Ware,' *O.C.S. Trans.*, 1936–37.

tended to run and that it was mixed with the native ore to give firm outlines. We have already seen that the same trouble was experienced by Persian potters, who often used black outlines as an edging to the blue. The Mohammedan blue was very precious in China, and we are told that in the reign of Chêng Tê it was carefully measured out to the workmen to prevent pilfering.

The Chinese references to the methods of use of Mohammedan blue are extremely vague. We have little information as to when it was actually used, what proportions of the native and imported ore were taken, or what methods of purification were adopted. Very few scientific analyses of the blue and white porcelain itself have been made. Some qualitative analyses on both Chinese and Persian blue glazes have been described by Young.[1] The Persian glazes were found to contain arsenic, while the early Chinese blue and white did not. Some recent investigations, not published, on both fourteenth century and K'ang Hsi blue and white, failed to reveal any arsenic in the former, although the amount of manganese was far less that that found in the K'ang Hsi pieces. The absence of arsenic does not prove conclusively that imported blue was not used, because arsenic is a volatile substance and may have evaporated at the high temperature reached in the firing.[2] The fourteenth century blue had a large amount of iron impurity which must have had a deleterious effect on the blue colour. It would be outside the scope of this book to discuss this complex question further, but it is important to stress that the problem of the Chinese use of cobalt in blue and white is one in which a thorough scientific examination would be of great value.

There can be no doubt that the Chinese potters were continually making experiments with different types of cobalt ore, purifying them by empirical methods. By the seventeenth century they had succeeded in producing, from the native ore, colours as fine as had been obtained earlier with imported ores.

* * * * * * *

Starting with the David vases as landmarks, we can now find a number of closely allied pieces and from them can attempt to trace the development of blue and white down to the classical reigns of the fifteenth century. The collections at Teheran and Istanbul, to which reference has already been made, provide the greater number of such pieces. But there are also many in western collections which, as a result of recent studies, are found also to belong to the early period

[1] W. J. Young, 'Discussion of some Analyses of Chinese Underglaze Blue and Underglaze Red,' *F.E.C.B.*, December 1949.

[2] Still more recent analyses have revealed the presence of small amounts of arsenic in a fourteenth century fragment.

of blue and white development. The studies of Shirae, Warren Cox[1] and Ayers[2] have drawn attention to the features of these pieces which connect them with the David vases, and distinguish them from the typical fifteenth century wares.

A vase at Istanbul (1) is of special importance because of its very close resemblance to the David vases. The main subject, a dragon in clouds and over waves, as well as the subsidiary bands of flower scrolls, waves and emblems, all present points of close resemblance. A number of bowls at Teheran and Istanbul (2) with markedly inverted lips, are decorated outside in bands that resemble those on the rather primitive pieces already described (3). The inside decoration of these bowls is of ducks or fishes in water plants, arranged in a symmetrical fashion. The stem cup in the Museum of Eastern Art, Oxford (4) is a fine example of this type.

The commonest pieces of early blue and white are large dishes with unglazed bases. The dishes are deep with a horizontal rim decorated with a border of diaper or waves, or more rarely with a flower scroll. The edge is sometimes plain and sometimes foliated. Inside this border, in the well of the dish, is a wider continuous scroll of flowers. This border is almost invariably repeated under the dish. The main subject of decoration, in a central panel, may consist of a landscape, with a rather haphazard collection of flowers and plants in great variety, sometimes with a *ch'i-lin* (5) phoenixes or pheasants in addition, ducks and water weeds, fishes and reeds (6), or more formal arrangements such as phoenixes in flower scrolls. In some dishes the design is quite formal (7), with clouds and waves enclosed in ogival borders and emblems in petal-shaped panels. In some of the dishes the inner border of flower scrolls and sometimes the central panel, consists of white flowers and leaves against a blue ground (8). In a few dishes the flowers are slightly raised in a moulded or carved design.

All the dishes just described have characteristics that associate them, in varying degrees, with the David vases and with each other, and justify the tentative assumption that they belong to the fourteenth century, although they cannot yet be placed in any sort of order. The characteristics that distinguish them from the typical fifteenth-century dishes may be seen by comparing the floral border of Plate 8B with that of the Hsüan Tê dish in Plate 16. The spiky flowers and leaves of the former and the way in which the scroll is confined, almost

[1] S. Shirae and Warren E. Cox, 'The Earliest Blue and White Wares of China,' *F.E.C.B.*, September 1949 and March 1950.
[2] J. Ayers, 'Early Chinese Blue and White,' *Oriental Art*, Vol. 3, No. 4.

(1) *Plate* 7; (2) *Plate* 8A; (3) *Plates* 1C, 5; (4) *Plates* 9A, 9B; (5) *Plate* 8B; (6) *Plate* 10; (7) *Plate* 11; (8) *Plate* 12.

as it were forcibly, within bounds, contrast with the rounded flowers and leaves and the more flowing scroll of the latter. The wave borders, when they appear on the earlier type of dish (1), are of vigorous serpentine form, with feathery spray emerging from them, while in the later dishes (2) they are more formal and symmetrical.

One of the most common type of dish is that decorated with a bunch of lotus flowers and leaves, tied with a ribbon. There are a dozen or more dishes with this decoration in the Teheran collection alone.[1] Most of them, including the fine example shown in Plates 13A, 13B, would be regarded as belonging to the fifteenth century. But Gray[2] has suggested that the pattern on a Syrian dish excavated at Hama and dating from the late fourteenth century is derived from a Chinese dish of this type. It is possible, therefore, that this type was made over a long period stretching back to the fourteenth century. The plates with grape vines (3) seem to have been almost as popular as those with a bunch of flowers. A less common type is decorated with fruiting melons (4). There are a few particularly large dishes, more than twenty-two inches in diameter, in the collection at Istanbul, one of which was exhibited at the Chinese Art Exhibition in 1935.[3] These belong to the early fifteenth century. An even larger dish, just under thirty inches in diameter and with the Hsüan Tê mark has been illustrated in the *Kokka*.[4] The technical achievement of making these large pieces shows what a complete mastery the Chinese had reached in the manufacture of porcelain by the beginning of the fifteenth century. Mention should also be made of some small foliated dishes with a raised rim suitable to support a cup.[5] Some of these may belong to the fourteenth century.

One of the most popular types of vase in China from late Sung times to the eighteenth century was that which is known today as *mei p'ing*, a vase of baluster shape with a short narrow neck. This type of vase was used in later times to hold a spray of flowering plum blossom.[6]

[1] Pope, *Harvard Journal of Asiatic Studies*, Plate 1.

[2] Gray, 'Blue and White Vessels in Persian Miniatures of the Fourteenth and Fifteenth Centuries Re-examined,' *O.C.S. Trans.*, 1948–49.

[3] See Jenyns, *Ming Pottery and Porcelain*, Plate 23B and Pope, 'Some Blue and White in Istanbul,' *O.C.S. Trans.*, 1950–51, Plate 11.

[4] *Kokka*, No. 711. Illustrated also in *Ming Blue and White and Enamelled Porcelain*, edited by the Nihon Tōzi Kyōkai, Plate 2.

[5] *Philadelphia Museum Bulletin*, No. 223, Plates, 24, 25.

[6] The references to this type of vase as *mei p'ing* do not seem to go further back than the early nineteenth century. Sir Percival David has referred me to a manuscript of the Chia Ch'ing period, which contains the earliest known reference. In the Chia Ching lists (see pp. 32, 33) this type of vase may be that described as *t'an* (large wine vessel), or *hua p'ing*.

(1) *Plates* 11, 12; (2) *Plate* 14; (3) *Plate* 14; (4) *Plate* 15.

But many of the earlier vases are fitted with a cap in the shape of a truncated cone (1) and this suggests that they were used as containers of liquid. The octagonal vase with panel decoration in the Mayer collection (2) has fourteenth-century characteristics, as has one in the Clark collection (3) decorated freely with flower scrolls which might be thought to represent paeonies, were it not for the tendrils. Some of the vases are decorated with human figures in landscapes (4), a subject that rarely, if ever, appears on the dishes. The figures with their dresses and ribbons streaming in the wind are vigorously and attractively drawn. The type persisted up to the end of the fifteenth century and indeed copies of these early vases are known with Chia Ching and Wan Li marks.

Almost as common as the *mei p'ing* vases were the massive jars (*kuan*), no doubt used as containers of food. Two early examples are shown in Plates 20 and 21. A study of these two jars, so much alike in shape and in the arrangement of the bands of decoration, but different in the technique of drawing, illustrates the difficulty of the exact dating of fourteenth-century blue and white. The drawing on the Hobart jar has some points of resemblance to that on the rectangular flask formerly in the Eumorfopoulos collection (5). Several flasks of this type, in the collections at Teheran[1] and Istanbul[2] provide strong evidence of fourteenth-century characteristics. Some of them, from the style of drawing of the waves and of the lotus scrolls on the sides, appear to be earlier than the Eumorfopoulos flask, and it seems possible that this shape, with a similar pattern of decoration, persisted for about half a century. We may tentatively place the Hobart jar and the Eumorfopoulos flask towards the end of the century and the jar in the Museum of Eastern Art earlier. The fine jar, decorated with ducks and water weeds, formerly in the Raphael collection (6), may also be placed in the earlier group. The drawing of this jar is highly individualistic and has been compared with that of the Yüan painter Ch'ien Hsüan.[3] The treatment of the pendant lotus leaves is particularly fine.

The vase and cover in the Toronto Museum (7) shows a close approach to the Imperial Hsüan Tê style. The decoration has a mixture of naturalism and formality, not uncommon at this time,

[1] Bahrami, 'Chinese Porcelains from Ardebilin the Teheran Museum,' *O.C.S. Trans.*, 1949–50.
[2] Pope, 'Fourteenth-Century Blue and White,' *Freer Gallery of Art Occasional Papers*, Vol. 2, No. 1.
[3] J. Ayers, 'Early Chinese Blue and White,' *Oriental Art*, Vol. 3, No. 4.

(1) *Plate* 19; (2) *Plate* 18; (3) *Plate* 17; (4) *Plate* 19; (5) *Plate* 24. (6) *Plate* 22A; (7) *Plate* 23.

which is not in the least incongruous. The large bowl with horizontal flange in the Melbourne Museum (1) has a shape copied from Persian metal ware.[1][2] In this piece the accidental effect of dots in the outlines seems to have been deliberately accentuated, a feature generally only to be found in late copies.[3]

[1] Gray, 'Influence of Near Eastern Metal Work on Chinese Ceramics,' *O.C.S. Trans.*, 1941–42.

[2] A bowl of similar shape, with the Hsüan Tê mark, is illustrated in Kushi, *Early Ming Chinese Porcelain*, Plate 17.

[3] But the fact that the dots, when they occur on sloping surfaces, are always found below the outlines, suggests that they are not artificial. The work recently initiated by Miss Medley (see reference on p. xvii) maybe expected to throw light on this feature.

(1) *Plate* 22B.

4

CLASSICAL REIGNS OF THE FIFTEENTH CENTURY

The blue and white discussed in the last chapter leads to the classical wares of the fifteenth century, always regarded in China as the outstanding period for blue and white. The most important reigns are those of Yung Lo (1403–1424), Hsüan Tê (1426–1435) and Ch'êng Hua (1465–1487). The last reign of the century Hung Chih (1488–1505) has not the same high reputation as the other reigns but the marked pieces that have survived are of high quality.

Mention should be made of a few pieces that are known bearing the mark of the first Ming Emperor Hung Wu (1368–1398). These are small saucers decorated with sages in landscapes in a number of different patterns,[1] which were at one time thought likely to belong to the period of the mark. But it is now clear that they have none of the qualities of early blue and white, although the individual quality of the painting makes them difficult to date exactly. Such dishes are known with the Chêng Tê mark[2] and they may very well belong to this period. They may be copies of fourteenth-century prototypes but if so these prototypes have still to be found.

Of the fifteenth century reigns, no pieces of blue and white of Imperial quality with the Yung Lo mark are known. Some bowls, decorated outside with a landscape, sometimes with the addition of a long poem, and with a heavily constructed foot, bearing the four character mark of Yung Lo are known.[3] One such bowl is known with the T'ien Ch'i mark,[4] which supports the view, which is generally accepted, that they belong to the seventeenth century.

It has been the custom to attribute unmarked pieces of blue and white of Imperial quality to the Yung Lo period, particularly when there are similar pieces with the Hsüan Tê mark, but there seems to be no justification for this. Such unmarked pieces were no doubt made

[1] See *Philadelphia Museum Bulletin*, No. 223, No. 149, and *Exhibition of Blue and White Porcelain*, London, 1953–54, Nos 211, 212.

[2] Kushi, *Early Ming Chinese Porcelain*, Plate 79.

[3] Brankston, *Early Ming Wares of Ching-tê Chên*, Plate 33.

[4] *Exhibition of Blue and White Porcelain*, London, 1953–54, No. 216.

21

during the Hsüan Tê period as well as before and after. We have thought it best to regard the Yung Lo period as a stage in the development from the fourteenth-century wares to the marked Imperial wares of Hsüan Tê. No doubt some of the later pieces among those described in the last Chapter belong to the Yung Lo period.

Many of the Imperial Hsüan Tê pieces are straight developments of familiar types. We have already referred to a dish with unglazed base and Hsüan Tê mark (1), a dish typical of those exported in large quantities to the Near East.

Among the most important marked pieces are the two very large *mei p'ing* vases, decorated with five-clawed dragons, in the William Rockhill Nelson Gallery of Art, Kansas City,[1] and a fine large jar, similarly decorated with three-clawed dragons (2) in the Metropolitan Museum, New York. The vases and jar all bear the four-character mark *Hsuan Te nien chih*, which is unusual with authentic pieces of this reign. The large jar (3), with its bold decoration of lotus scrolls, has the more usual six-character mark on the shoulder. There are also some heavily constructed fruit bowls bearing designs of flower scrolls, dragons or fruiting sprays with the mark below the rim (4). The large bottle with dragons in waves (5), although unmarked, is of Imperial quality and probably belongs to the first half of the fifteenth century.[2]

The pieces just described are massive pieces intended for heavy use. There are, however, a number of more delicately potted bowls, stem cups and small vases which must have been made for intimate Imperial use. At any rate, pieces of this kind are not found in the large export collections at Teheran and Istanbul. The two stem cups in Plates 27A, 27B are fine examples of this type. Other examples are the delicately potted foliated bowl in Plate 27C and the bowl in Plate 28A. The latter, although unmarked, is of the same high quality as the marked pieces. The central design on the dish of Plate 28B is a miniature version of that found on a well-known export type. A dish (6) with the uncommon decoration of a dragon in waterweeds has two dragons in slip decoration bordering the central pattern and this provides a connecting link with the earlier *shu-fu* decoration. The similar dish with the Hung Chih mark (7) has no slip decoration.

The flask (8) or 'moon vase' is a type that is well represented in the Near-Eastern collections. Another moon vase, in the collection

---

[1] *Philadelphia Museum Bulletin*, No. 223, Nos. 48, 49.
[2] Some points of resemblance with Plate 25 may be noted.

---

(1) *Plate* 16; (2) *Plate* 25; (3) *Colour Plate* B; (4) *Plate* 26A; (5) *Plate* 26B; (6) *Plate* 29A; (7) *Plate* 29B; (8) *Plate* 30A.

D. CHÊNG TÊ PERIOD. DIAM. 6.5 in.
See page 29

of Mrs. Sedgwick,[1] has an incised mark of Alamgir, a name of the Mogul Emperor Aurangzeb and the date AH 1070 (1659–1660). These flasks can be dated, on grounds of style, to the early part of the fifteenth century. They were copied extensively during the eighteenth century, a common subject of decoration being birds on a prunus tree. The small jar and cover (1) bears a delightful decoration of growing plants, including the carnation, which also occurs on a large flask at Istanbul. Another form of flask, in the shape of a double gourd, is also found in Near-Eastern collections. They are unmarked, but similar flasks, of finer quality (2) have the Hsüan Tê mark and are undoubtedly Imperial pieces. Small bowls in the shape of a lotus pod (*lien tzŭ*) sometimes have the Hsüan Tê mark (3) and are sometimes unmarked. The leys jar (4) is of a shape that seems to have first occurred in the fifteenth century. We shall see later pieces in this shape in the second half of the century and in the reign of Chêng Tê.

* * * * * * *

The second classical reign in the fifteenth century is that of Ch'êng Hua (1465–1487). The period of thirty years between the end of Hsüan Tê's reign and the accession of Ch'êng Hua is almost a blank in the history of porcelain. Hsüan Tê was succeeded by his eldest son, Ying Tsung, a boy nine years old, who reigned for thirteen years with the title of Chêng T'ung (1436–1449), under his mother's guidance. The Ming Annals[2] record that during this period the eunuchs under Wang Chen gained virtual control and the Court was split into contending parties. The Mongols, taking advantage of the internal dissensions, invaded the country in 1449, defeated the Emperor's troops and captured him. Chêng T'ung was succeeded by his younger brother, who reigned under the title Ching T'ai (1450–1456). In 1457 Ying Tsung returned and resumed the throne under the title T'ien Shun. He died in 1464 and was succeeded by his eldest son Hsien Tsung who reigned under the title Ch'êng Hua.

We have little information from the Chinese records on what porcelain was being made during these thirty years. The records of Kiangsi say that the manufacture of Imperial porcelain ceased at the end of the Hsüan Tê period and was resumed in the first year of T'ien Shun (1457). It is also stated in the *Yü chang ta shih chi* that the amount

[1] *International Exhibition of Chinese Art*, 1935, No. 1470 and *Exhibition of Chinese Blue and White*, London, 1953–54, No. 44.

[2] *Ming shih (Pên chi)*. See Brankston, *Early Ming Wares of Ching-tê Chên*, p. 35.

(1) *Plate* 30B; (2) *Plate* 31A; (3) *Plate* 30C; (4) *Plate* 31B.

of porcelain made in the fifth year of Ching T'ai (1454) was one third of that of former times.

No pieces of blue and white of Imperial quality bearing the reign marks of any of the three Emperors Chêng T'ung, Ching T'ai or T'ien Shun have yet come to light. A few small bowls of poor quality with the mark of T'ien Shun are known, but they are not sufficiently distinctive to be ascribed with certainty to any particular Ming period. The reign of Ching T'ai is noted for its cloisonné and a number of fine pieces bear the six-character *nien hao* of this reign.[1] Many of them are accepted as belonging to the Ching T'ai period. Two pieces of white porcelain of fine quality bearing the mark of T'ien Shun are known. One is a dish in the David Foundation with unglazed base and foot rim typical of the fifteenth century, with moulded decoration of phoenixes and bearing the four-character incised mark. The quality of this, in material and finish, is equivalent to that of the usual large fifteenth-century blue and white dishes. A stem cup, in the possession of Mr. Peter Boode, with the six-character mark *Ta Ming T'ien Shun nien tsao*, finely decorated in slip with animals under the white glaze, is as fine in quality as the best Imperial pieces of Hsüan Tê. It has every indication of belonging to the fifteenth century.

The fine cloisonné of Ching T'ai and the two pieces of white porcelain of T'ien Shun show that, at any rate in two of the three reigns between Hsüan Tê and Ch'êng Hua, works of art of the finest quality were being produced, and it is almost unbelievable that fine pieces of blue and white, that had reached such distinction in the reign of Hsüan Tê, were not being made then. It is possible that many fine unmarked pieces were made, some in the Hsüan Tê style and some in that which we are now beginning to associate with the second half of the fifteenth century. We also cannot rule out the possibility that some of the pieces in fifteenth-century style bearing the Hsüan Tê mark were made in this period. The contention has often been made that the large number of such pieces that must have been made, in view of the many hundreds that are known today, could not have been made in Hsüan Tê's short reign of nine years.[2] A critical examination of these pieces suggests that the majority of them, with clearly defined fifteenth-century characteristics, were not made in later Ming times and are not eighteenth-century copies. There is a great reluctance among Chinese connoisseurs to accept the view that the *nien hao* could have been copied a few years after an Emperor's

[1] Jenyns, 'The Problem of Chinese Cloisonné Enamels,' *O.C.S. Trans.*, 1949–50
[2] Reitlinger and Button, 'Early Ming Blue and White,' *Burlington Magazine* January, March 1948.

death, although there does not seem to be any embargo mentioned in any of the Chinese writings. The question as to whether pieces bearing the Hsüan Tê mark were actually made in this period must be left open until further evidence is obtained.

*   *   *   *   *   *   *

The porcelain of the reign of Ch'êng Hua itself also presents some puzzling features. It is by far the most difficult of the classical Ming reigns. The best known pieces are so-called 'palace bowls', decorated with scrolling patterns of flowers such as lilies, poppies and fruiting melons. These bowls mark a distinct break with the earlier fifteenth-century tradition and before we consider them it will be of advantage to examine the smaller group of pieces with the Ch'êng Hua mark decorated in Hsüan Tê style. They provide a connecting link between the pieces of Hsüan Tê on the one hand and Hung Chih on the other. A dish decorated with the three friends, the pine, bamboo and plum, and bearing the Ch'êng Hua mark, is shown with a similar dish with the Hsüan Tê mark in Plates 32A, 32B. Both are in typical fifteenth-century style, but the dish with the Ch'êng Hua mark shows less contrast and less 'heaped and piled' effect in the blue decoration. The drawing is inferior and the trees are spaced with less skill. It has strong claims, however, to belong to the period of the mark. The deterioration of the drawing, by Hsüan Tê standards, is typical of the Ch'êng Hua reign and we must learn to accept it if our judgment of this period is not to be warped.[1] This type of dish, with the three friends, was copied in a number of Ch'ing reigns, as we shall see later. There are also, with the Ch'êng Hua mark, dishes and bowls decorated with dragons in floral scrolls closely following the Hsüan Tê pattern. The drawing of dragons on a bowl in the David Foundation (1), also in the earlier tradition, is very close to that on the later dishes and bowls bearing the Hung Chih mark. The dish (2) bearing the eight Buddhist emblems supported on lotus flowers is probably also based on a Hsüan Tê original,[2] while one decorated with phoenixes in lotus scrolls (3) also has its earlier counterparts.[3] Although all these pieces show unmistakable signs of fifteenth-century painting, we can

[1] Brankston refers to the uncertain drawing of the Ch'êng Hua period. See *Early Ming Wares of Ching-tê Chên*, p. 47.

[2] The decoration appears on a 'narcissus bowl', No. 89, *Exhibition of Chinese Blue and White*, London, 1953–54. A bowl with this decoration is mentioned by Brankston, *Early Wares of Ching-tê Chên*, p. 22.

[3] Cf. *Philadelphia Museum Bulletin*, No. 70, Brankston, *loc. cit.* Plate 21B and *Exhibition of Chinese Blue and White*, London, Nos. 61, 63.

(1) Plate 33A; (2) Plate 33B; (3) Plate 34.

trace the emergence of a new technique, which finally resulted in the disappearance of the 'heaped and piled' effect, so characteristic of the earlier wares, by the end of the century.

The so-called 'palace bowls',[1] as we have said, mark a distinct break with the fifteenth-century tradition. They are decorated in a lighter and more delicate style, without the usual 'heaped and piled' effect, and are covered with a smoother and thinner glaze, with little sign of the orange skin texture of the earlier wares. The subjects of decoration are scrolls of lilies, lotus, poppies or paeonies, chrysanthemums, or sprays of fruiting melons (1). The delicate painting of some of these bowls has great charm, in spite of a lack of decision in the drawing, very different from the boldness of the earlier blue and white. This type of decoration was easier for the eighteenth-century potters to copy than the Hsüan Tê style and considerable difficulty is experienced at times in distinguishing the earlier pieces from the later. Two examples of Ch'êng Hua blue and white are shown with Yung Chêng copies in Plates 36, 37. As far as the two bowls in Plate 36 are concerned, the drawing of the earlier bowl is better arranged and more skilfully done than that of the later one, but such differences in drawing are not always so apparent. One distinction between the earlier and later pieces lies in the method of application of the blue pigment. Although the bolder and more vigorous style of the earlier part of the century had been abandoned by the time of Ch'êng Hua, the method of applying the pigment in a mottled wash still remained. This contrasts with the even, mechanical application of the Yung Chêng copies. The differences, which can be seen in the illustrations, are more apparent in the actual pieces.

The marks of the Ch'êng Hua period also differ a great deal from those of the earlier and later reigns. They are freely and loosely painted with a rather wet brush. The calligraphy is generally inferior to that of the Hsüan Tê period and the later period Hung Chih.

* * * * * * *

Very few pieces are known of blue and white bearing the mark of Hung Chih. With the exception of the important vase dated 1496 in the David Foundation (2), all the known types are decorated with Imperial dragons in one form or another. Three types of dish, decorated on the front with one dragon, two dragons and three clouds

[1] The use of the term 'palace bowl' for this type of bowl is curious. The bowls and dishes decorated with dragons and phoenixes, undoubtedly made for the palace, seem to be excluded from the term.

(1) *Plates* 35A, 35B; (2) *Plate* 38.

respectively are shown in Plate 39. They all have the same decoration, two dragons in clouds, underneath (1). A dish with a dragon in water weeds, with its Hsüan Tê prototype, has already been referred to (2). Bowls with decoration similar to that on the Ch'êng Hua bowl in Plate 33A are also known. Although the colour of the blue is greyish all these pieces are of particularly high quality and are marked in excellent calligraphy (3).

There are a number of fine unmarked pieces, some of which approach Imperial quality, that may be attributed to the second half of the fifteenth century. These include a fine leys jar (4), which may well be somewhat earlier than the Ch'êng Hua period, a large bowl (5) and stem cup (6), both attractively decorated with figures in a landscape. The brush holder (7), in which the style of decoration of the flower scrolls resembles that of the dated David vase, probably belongs to the end of the century.

A series of dishes decorated with floral sprays, some in blue and white and others in blue and yellow, the yellow enamel having been added in a second firing, are of interest in showing the changes of style from the reign of Hsüan Tê to that of Chêng Tê (8). The dish in this series with the Ch'êng Hua mark (9) provides a useful connecting link with the 'palace bowls' in its style of decoration, and the one with the Hung Chih mark (10) seems to be the only additional type known of underglaze blue painting with the mark of this period.

By the end of the fifteenth century a new style of decoration in blue and white had arisen. The method of painting in bold splashes of colour had been replaced by one in which the outlines were carefully drawn and the spaces filled in with a uniform wash. The first reign of the sixteenth century, Chêng Tê, saw the final disappearance of the old style.

---

(1) *Plate* 39D; (2) *Plates* 29A, 29B; (3) *Plate* 39D; (4) *Plate* 41B; (5) *Plate* 40B; (6) *Plate* 41A; (7) *Plate* 40A; (8) *Plates* 42 A, B, C, D; (9) *Plate* 42B; (10) *Plate* 42C.

5

THE SIXTEENTH CENTURY

The reign of Chêng Tê (1506–1521), together with the previous reign Hung Chih, marks the final transition from the fifteenth-century style to that of the sixteenth. Much of the porcelain of Chêng Tê has qualities distinct from those of the succeeding reigns Chia Ching (1522–1566), Lung Ch'ing (1567–1572) and Wan Li (1573–1617) which are generally regarded as the typical sixteenth-century reigns.

One of the most interesting groups of Chêng Tê blue and white consists of what are known as Mohammedan wares. These pieces are decorated with inscriptions in either Arabic or Persian. The characters of the inscriptions are enclosed in cartouches surrounded by formal foliage scrolls drawn rather stiffly by means of thick outlines carefully filled in with a wash. The scrolls are described by Chinese writers as *hui hui wen* (Mohammedan scrolls) and seem to derive from Persian sources.

These pieces are made in a great variety of shapes, there being few bowls and dishes. They include articles for the writing table such as brush rests, ink slabs and boxes with covers as well as vases of various shapes and hat stands. Although stoutly constructed they are made of porcelain of fine quality. The colour of the blue is good and the glaze is thick with a pronounced greenish tinge. They are all marked with the six-character mark *Ta Ming Chêng Tê nien chih* in very good calligraphy.

The box and cover (1) in the Royal Ontario Museum of Archaeology bears the two inscriptions in Arabic 'Strive for excellence in penmanship, for it is one of the keys of livelihood,' and 'A fool finds no contentment.' It would seem that these inscriptions formed a series of stock phrases, for we find the first on the upper part of an ink slab in the British Museum,[1] while the second is found on the lower part of

[1] R. L. Hobson, *Handbook of the Pottery and Porcelain of the Far East*, 1948, Fig. 84.

(1) *Plate* 43A.

a box in the Seligman collection,[1] The vase (1), which at various times has been described as a lamp or candle holder,[2] bears an inscription in Persian 'Preserve our faith from danger', while the similar piece in hexagonal form (2) also has a Persian inscription 'I was loitering in a deserted place when suddenly I found a treasure'. A number of pen rests, in two different forms, are to be found in Western collections. The one illustrated (3) bears the simple inscription in Persian 'Pen rest'. The large desk screen (4) has three verses in Arabic from Chapter 72 of the Koran. The hat stand (5), one of a pair in the British Museum, bears the inscription in Arabic 'O God, may his country be safe and his progeny be preserved'. These two hat stands have suffered from being in a fire; the glaze is dulled and there are discolourations including some red patches which may well have been caused by the proximity of bronzes in the fire. The circular box and cover (6) is a piece in typical Mohammedan style although it does not bear an inscription.

Students of Chinese ceramic history have naturally been very interested in the purpose for which this porcelain of fine quality was made. Was it made for export to the Near East or for the use of Mohammedans in China? Basil Gray has expressed the view,[3] based on a study of Chinese and Persian metal and ceramic forms, that the porcelain was made for use in China. Most of the pieces, such as the articles for the writing table, would indeed be of little interest to the Near-Eastern people, and it is significant that the only pieces that have been found in the Near East are a few bowls and dishes, which, as we have said, represent only a small proportion of these wares.

There is evidence that the influence of the Mohammedan eunuchs in the reign of Chêng Tê was very strong. He was a child when he came to the throne and he is said to have come under the influence of the eunuchs, who encouraged him in a life of vice while they managed state affairs in their own interests. 'Ali Ekber, a Moslem merchant from eastern Turkey, paid a visit to China in 1505 and wrote a long account of what he saw there, which is generally accepted as reliable. He tells us that most of the officials of the court were eunuchs, among whom were many Moslems. He also says that the young Emperor Chêng Tê was believed to have embraced the Moslem faith.

[1] *O.C.S. Exhibition, Blue and White Porcelain*, 1946, No. 57, Plate III.
[2] The resemblance of these pieces to the metal lamps or candle holders is very small, and it is difficult to see how they could be used as such.
[3] Gray, 'The Influence of Near Eastern Metalwork on Chinese Ceramics, *O.C.S. Trans.*, 1941–42.

(1) *Plate* 43B; (2) *Plate* 43C; (3) *Plate* 44A; (4) *Plate* 45; (5) *Plate* 44B; (6) *Colour Plate* D.

This, however, is not recorded in the Ming Annals and it may well be that 'Ali Ekber, as an ardent Mohammedan, made the wish the father to the thought.

We may thus picture, in the reign of Chêng Tê, a powerful group of Moslem eunuchs who were able to get porcelain made for their exclusive use in the Imperial factory and bearing the *nien hao* of the Emperor. The Mohammedan wares were made for use in the Moslems' offices and not, generally, if we may judge from the small number of bowls and dishes that survive, for eating and drinking. Many of these Moslems would be of Near-Eastern descent and would be familiar with the Persian language for ordinary use as well as with Arabic for religious use. We need not be surprised therefore that both Persian and Arabic are used in the inscriptions on Mohammedan wares.

When Chia Ching, who was a believer in Taoism and intolerant of other religious creeds, came to the throne he made a clean sweep of the Mohammedan eunuchs. It would be expected, therefore, that the Mohammedan wares would cease to be made at the end of Chêng Tê's reign and in fact we do not know of any bearing the mark of Chia Ching. There are, of course, many pieces belonging to the later Ming reigns bearing Arabic or Persian inscriptions, but these are in quite another class from the Chêng Tê Mohammedan wares, which stand in splendid isolation.

The second class of Chêng Tê blue and white is decorated with Imperial dragons in lotus scrolls. It is confined to dishes of various sizes (1), bowls, ewers and leys jars (*Cha-tou*) (2). These are finely potted and the decoration, although overcrowded, is well drawn, generally in a greyish blue. They invariably bear the four-character mark *Chêng Tê nien chih*. There are also with this mark some large baluster vases (3), with a cylindrical neck and flared mouth, decorated with flower scrolls.

The marking of Chêng Tê porcelain presents some puzzling features. A number of types, clearly of Imperial quality, bear the four-character mark including, in addition to the pieces already described, those decorated with green dragons on a yellow ground and a group of pieces with three-coloured enamels. The Mohammedan pieces, those decorated with green dragons on a white ground and a set of large dishes with blue floral sprays on a yellow ground always bear the six-character mark, as do most of the plain yellow dishes.

No satisfactory explanation for the use of the four-character mark on Chêng Tê pieces has been put forward. As we have seen, the four-character mark appears on a few important Hsüan Tê pieces of blue

(1) *Plate* 46A; (2) *Plate* 46B; (3) *Plate* 47.

E. SECOND HALF OF SIXTEENTH CENTURY. DIAM. 5.5 in.
Mr. R. F. A. Riesco
See pages 35, 36

and white but few other examples are known of the use in the Ming dynasty of the four-character reign mark on pieces of fine quality.

There is also, in this period, a small group of jars which is of special interest because it enables us to date a large number of unmarked pieces with similar shapes and decoration. The jars are small and of oviform shape in elevation, but may be round, square, hexagonal or octagonal in section. They are decorated in a pale blue with such subjects as emblems (1), phoenixes in lotus sprays (2) and children at play (3). The mark is four-charactered in the form *Chêng Tê nien tsao*. There are also polychrome jars of this type. The jars are well potted and some of them, except that the blue is pale rather than dark, closely resemble pieces of Imperial quality of the next reign Chia Ching. The Chêng Tê jars are almost certainly non-Imperial, although they were no doubt made in one of the Ching-tê Chên potteries. There are many similar jars to these either having no mark, or more rarely bearing the mark of Hsüan Tê. This enables us with some certainty to say that the mark of Hsüan Tê was being used early in the sixteenth century.

Reference has been made to some small dishes, decorated with sages in landscapes, generally bearing the mark of Hung Wu, but sometimes that of Chêng Tê, which may belong to the latter period. A dish of finer quality, decorated in a dark purplish blue with birds on flowering and fruiting branches, and with the four-character Chêng Tê mark, was shown at the Oriental Ceramic Society's blue and white exhibition, London, in 1953–54.[1] It has strong claims to belong to the period of its mark.

* * * * * * *

The blue and white of the reign of Chia Ching (1522–1566) has always been prized for the brilliance of its blue decoration. In spite of the use of the imported 'Mohammedan blue' in the earlier Ming reigns, the potters were rarely able to avoid a touch of greyness in the blue. In the reign of Chia Ching the potters succeeded, partly by the use of the imported colour and partly no doubt by improved methods of purifying the cobalt ore, in getting the brilliant dark purplish blue which is regarded as typical of this period.

The Chinese were usually tolerant in religious matters and we generally find Buddhism, Taoism and Confucianism flourishing side by side. But Chia Ching, in his attachment to Taoism, was intolerant of other religious creeds and made great efforts to suppress them. We are

[1] No. 133, Plate 11c.

---

(1) *Plate* 48A; (2) *Plate* 48B; (3) *Plate* 48C.

told, for example, that in 1536 the Buddhist temples in Peking were destroyed by his order. Under these circumstances we find, as we should expect, a strong Taoist influence in the subjects chosen for the decoration of Chia Ching blue and white. The emblems of immortality, such as the pine tree, deer and crane are used in various combinations. A favourite device is the peach tree with its trunk twisted into the form of the symbol of long life (*shou*) (1). The eight immortals and other Taoist figures are often used. At the same time many of the subjects used in earlier reigns were continued. They include the dragon (2), phoenix, flower scrolls and children at play (3).

We get a good idea of the great variety and quantity of blue and white porcelain made for the Chia Ching court from the lists prepared every year for the supply of pieces for palace use. These are given in the *Fou-liang hsien chih*, from the eighth year of the reign of Chia Ching onwards (1529). It is there stated that all records of earlier years had been burned. This is true of the provincial records, but copies of these were sent regularly by the Governor of the province to Peking, where they have been preserved. Much of the information has been incorporated in the *Ming shih lu*, a work which is mostly still in manuscript in Peking. In it there is given a day to day record of all happenings as reported to the palace during the various reigns of the Ming dynasty. But these voluminous palace records have never been indexed or classified and they would have to be studied by a large team of Chinese scholars before the parts relevant to porcelain manufacture could be extracted.

The earlier lists in the *Fou-liang hsien chih*[1] are short and lacking in detail, and it is not until the thirteenth year of Chia Ching's reign (1534), in which over six thousand bowls, cups and dishes are recorded, that we can recognise the types of decoration used. The first comprehensive list is that of the twenty-first year (1542), where we find described the jars (*kuan*) decorated with lions playing with embroidered balls, peacocks with tree paeonies (*mu-tan*) and the eight Taoist genii, as well as dragon and phoenix bowls, all types which are familiar to collectors today. In 1544 the enormous order of 1,340 table services comprising over 35,000 pieces was placed, while in the year 1554 we find that over one hundred thousand pieces were required for the court.[2] The extensive lists for the years 1546 and

[1] The only copy of the *Fou-liang hsien chih* known in the west is in the Bibliothèque Nationale, Paris. This is a copy of the last edition, published in 1823, and is defective. It is discussed in *Artibus Asiae*, Vol. XII, 3, 1949 by Sir Percival David, to whom I am indebted for translations of the earlier Chia Ching lists.

[2] Bushell, *Oriental Ceramic Art*, 1899, p. 226.

(1) *Plate* 49; (2) *Plate* 50A; (3) *Plate* 50B.

1554 have been given in detail by Bushell[1] and Hobson.[2]

A typical jar (*kuan*) and cover of square section decorated with dragons in flower scrolls (1) follows closely the Chêng Tê jars (2). The jar with Taoist figures (3) bears the cyclical date 1561 and so gives us some idea of the style followed towards the end of the reign.

*   *   *   *   *   *   *

The first direct exportation of Chinese porcelain to Europe occurred early in the sixteenth century. In 1498 Vasco da Gama sailed round the Cape of Good Hope and landed in India, and this led to the opening of a trade route between Portugal and the far east. A Portuguese settlement was made at Malacca which served as a base from which expeditions were made to China. The first expedition took place in 1514 and others followed, first to the large city of Canton, afterwards to the ports of Changchow and Ch'üanchow in the province of Fukien and finally to Ning Po in the province of Chekiang. In the first few years the relations between the two countries were amicable but as a result of outrages committed by the Portuguese fleet under Simão d'Andrade trade relations were broken off by the Chinese in 1524. From then onwards for a long time trade was carried on under cover, partly through intermediaries but also by smuggling, in which the Chinese inhabitants on the coasts of Fukien and Chekiang connived with the Portuguese to carry on a substantial trade in spite of the Imperial edict. It was not until 1554 that trade relations were officially re-established, when the Portuguese were allowed to form a settlement at Macao close to Canton. This became a trading centre of great importance and it was, until towards the end of the Ming dynasty, the main centre of European trade with China.[3]

The porcelain exported to Europe at this time was almost entirely blue and white. The Dominican friar Gaspar da Cruz, who left Portugal for the Far East in 1547, was the first European to describe something of the processes of manufacture of blue and white porcelain in China. In his book,[4] published in 1569, he describes the method of

[1] *Loc. cit.*, pp. 223–225.

[2] Hobson, *The Wares of the Ming Dynasty*, 1923.

[3] A full account of the trade relationships of the Chinese and Portuguese is given by T'ien-tse Chang, *Sino-Portuguese Trade from* 1514 *to* 1644, Leyden 1934.

[4] *Tratado em que se cotan muito por esteso a cousas da China co suas particularidades e asi de reyno de Ormuz*, Lisboa, 1569. This was translated into English, somewhat abbreviated, in *Hakluytus Posthumus*, or *Purchas his Pilgrims*, 1624. Reprinted 1906 by James MacLehose and Sons, Glasgow. Gaspar da Cruz' account is in Vol. XI.

(1) *Plate* 50A; (2) *Plates* 48B, 48C; (3) *Plate* 51.

purifying the clay and refers to the painting of blue under he glaze. In addition to the many pieces of unmarked blue and white exported at this time, there exist a few pieces with dated inscriptions in Portuguese. Two of these are bowls fitted with side handles or ears, of the same shape and bearing the Hsüan Tê mark, but differently decorated. The first has Mongolian horsemen on the outside and a central panel inside containing a sage seated in a landscape. The second is decorated outside with children at play and has inside a shield of arms, which has been identified as belonging to the ancient Portuguese family of Abreu. Each bowl bears the inscription 'Em tempo de Rero de Faria de 1541.[1] The first bowl belongs to Dr. de Castro e Brito and the second is in the Meseu Duca di Martina, Naples. Pero de Faria (Rero is a mistake of the Chinese artist) was a Portuguese adventurer of some importance, about whom a good deal has been recorded. As a young man he fought in naval battles against the Turks in the Mediterranean. He went to India round about 1505 and stayed in the East until his death in 1546. He was Governor of Malacca on two occasions, the second time in 1541, the date inscribed on the bowls. There can be no doubt that the bowls were made to his direct order, although the negotiations necessary must have taken place under difficult conditions, in view of the official ban on trade. We know that Fernão Mendez Pinto, the Portuguese writer and adventurer, was sent from Malacca to China at this time,[2] and he may very well have acted as the intermediary.[3]

These bowls provide convincing evidence of the type of porcelain that was being made for non-Imperial purposes in the middle of the sixteenth century. Except for their inscriptions, and for the shield of arms in the second bowl, the bowls are purely Chinese in design, even to the Hsüan Tê mark, and we may be sure that similar bowls, without the European appendages, were made for local use.

Another piece with a dated Portuguese inscription is a bottle, with the neck cut down, in the Victoria and Albert Museum, which bears the date 1557 (I). The inscription, in two rows, upside down, appears to be incomplete, but it states that the piece was made for Jorge Anrz (short for Anriques or Alvarez) in 1557.

[1] L. Keil, 'Porcelanas Chinesas do seculo XVI com inscrições em Portuguès, *Boletim da Academia Nacional de Belas-Artes*, Lisboa, 1942. See also *O.C.S. Trans.*, 1935–36, Plate 12.

[2] T'ien-tse Chang, *loc. cit.*

[3] His account of his adventures is given in his *Peregrinação*, published in 1614, about thirty years after his death. It is not regarded as entirely reliable. Congreve describes him in *Love for Love* as a 'liar of the first magnitude'.

(I) *Plate* 56A.

From this time onwards large and increasing quantities of porcelain were exported to Europe, first to Portugal and afterwards to Holland and other countries. These export wares will be discussed later, under the Wan Li period, to which no doubt the greater part of the pieces known today belong. But there are two non-Imperial pieces which probably belong to the end of the Chia Ching period which should be mentioned here. The first is a dish which is just an early and refined example of export ware (1). The second (2), a bowl bearing the inscription 'Elegant vessel for the President',[1] is as fine as anything produced during the Chia Ching period, although non-Imperial. Apart from its intrinsic beauty, it is of special interest because the design and drawing are so close to those of the export dish and so far from those of the conventional Imperial wares, This little bowl seems to presage the breaking away from Imperial control, which became complete at the end of Wan Li's reign and led to the Transition wares of the seventeenth century.

* * * * * * *

The porcelain of the short reign of Lung Ch'ing (1567–1572) has similar qualities to that of the previous and succeeding reigns of Chia Ching and Wan Li. The Imperial factory seems to have been closed during the earlier years of the reign, and a large order for more than a hundred thousand pieces was placed in 1571 because supplies for the palace had run short. Two typical pieces with the Lung Ch'ing mark are shown in Plates 52A and 52B.

* * * * * * *

The Imperial blue and white porcelain of the reign of Wan Li (1573–1619) tends to be somewhat overshadowed by that of Chia Ching. Although the typical Chia Ching types were repeated (3), the Wan Li blue only occasionally reached the brilliance of the earlier reign and the drawing tended to become perfunctory. The beds of fine clay, situated at Ma-ts'ang, were beginning to be used up in the reign of Chia Ching and by the time of Wan Li the potters had to go much further afield for the clay. Although a small proportion of the porcelain was still of very high quality, the difficulty of finding good clay resulted in a general lowering of standards. The stove jar (4), intended to contain a brazier, and perhaps originally fitted with a perforated lid,

---

[1] The President referred to is the President of the Six Boards. An alternative rendering of the inscription is 'Elegant vessel for the Terrace Pavilion'.

---

(1) *Plate* 57; (2) *Colour Plate* E; (3) *Plates* 53A, 53B; (4) *Plate* 54.

dates from the last year but one of Wan Li's reign.[1] The decoration is in a style that was popular in the reign of Chia Ching and so must have been followed for more than half a century. The standard of potting and decoration is decidedly lower than that of the earlier pieces in this style; this may be partly explained by the fact that the jar is a presentation piece to a temple.

As if to compensate for the deterioration of the standard Imperial wares, a new and lighter style of decoration in a silvery blue was developed (1). The small stem cup, unmarked, of a type accepted as fifteenth century less than thirty years ago,[2] is typical of a large number of delicately decorated pieces bearing the mark of either Hsüan Tê or Ch'êng Hua. These are some of the most charming pieces of this period. The small incense burner (2), dated 1612, and inscribed with the name of the potter Ch'êng,[3] is an example that seems to stand by itself. It is reminiscent of the Ch'êng Hua period but seems also to foreshadow the lighter styles of decoration of the K'ang Hsi and Yung Chêng periods.

The individual quality of some of the pieces of the second half of the sixteenth and the first half of the seventeenth centuries lends some support to the view that they were made by artist potters. There are many stories in the Chinese literature[4] about the skill of these potters and their imitations of the earlier wares, but at present we know of few pieces, such as the incense burner in Plate 55B, with the mark of an individual potter and there are no pieces of blue and white, as far as I am aware, that can be definitely attributed to any of the potters whose names are recorded in the T'ao Lu.

The supply of export pieces to Europe at this time must have been immense, if we may judge by the large number of pieces that have survived. These export wares were no doubt generally the coarser pieces of a class of porcelain made to meet the needs of the Chinese non-Imperial user. We have already noted two early refined pieces of this class (3) and a third later example (4) is delicately potted and painted in a clear silvery blue. The standard export pieces, as a rule, are much coarser. They are roughly finished with radial marks, caused by the slipping of the turning tool and colloquially known as

[1] Another jar, of rather different shape, from the same set, is in the Tokyo National Museum.

[2] Hobson, *The Wares of the Ming Dynasty*, p. 76.

[3] The piece is inscribed 'Wan Li jen tzü Ch'êng t'ao kuan chih', made by Ch'êng T'ao-kuan in the jen tzü year of Wan Li.

[4] Ching-tê Chên T'ao Lu. Translated by Geoffrey R. Sayer, pp. 46, 47.

(1) *Plate* 55A; (2) *Plate* 55B; (3) *Colour Plate* E and *Plate* 57; (4) *Plate* 55C.

'chatter marks', visible under the base and with coarse grit adhering to the foot rim. But they are skilfully and vigorously decorated with such subjects as ducks and water weeds (1), spotted deer (2) or landscapes, sometimes with human figures (3). A feature of many of them is the use of a twisted branch, no doubt intended to represent the character for longevity (*shou*), which encloses the deer or human figures (4). One fragile type of dish, possibly based on a metal prototype, with edges so thin that it is surprising that any have survived without damage, is generally decorated with a wide border of trophies alternating with flowering or fruiting sprays in panels, and with a central panel forming the main subject of decoration (5). The bowl and cover (6) is a complete example, not often to be found, of this type. The interior decoration, in which the panels are simplified, is a familiar feature of the bowls and dishes often to be seen in Dutch still life pictures of the early seventeenth century. This type of porcelain is known as *Kraak porselein*, from the Dutch term for the type of Portuguese ship from which the porcelain was first captured in 1603. This ship, the carrack *Catherina*, with a rich cargo of silk, porcelain and lacquered wares, was captured in the Straits of Malacca and taken to Amsterdam, where the spoil caused a great sensation. The goods were sold for over three million guilders. Kraak porcelain had a great influence on the development of European pottery, being extensively copied at Delft and other European potteries.

---

(1) *Plate* 56B; (2) *Plate* 58A, left; (3) *Plate* 58A, right; (4) *Plate* 58A, centre; (5) *Plate* 58A, right; (6) *Plate* 58B.

6

THE END OF THE MING
DYNASTY

Wan Li was the last great Emperor of the Ming dynasty. During his reign the throne was already being weakened by internal dissensions and attacks from outside, and after his death in 1619 the end of the dynasty was in sight. The subsequent reigns of T'ien Ch'i (1621–1627) and Ch'ung Chêng (1628–1643) were very unsettled, the country being under continuous attacks from the Manchus, who succeeded in setting up a new dynasty in 1644. Revolts against the new dynasty were frequent and were not finally suppressed until K'ang Hsi came to the throne in 1662.

The period between 1620 and 1662[1] is generally known as the 'Transition Period' and although very little porcelain that could be called Imperial was produced during this time, it was, ceramically, of great interest. The interest lies in the non-Imperial wares, bearing no marks of the period, but occasionally bearing the marks of previous Ming reigns.

In the absence of any record of the Imperial and other potteries after the reign of Wan Li, we can only judge the wares of this period by examining the few marked and dated pieces and those pieces bearing datable European silver mounts. There are a number of small dishes, simply but attractively decorated in a dull greyish blue, with a little overglaze decoration added in red, green and yellow, belonging to the second quarter of the seventeenth century. Some of them bear the four-character mark of T'ien Ch'i. Others are unmarked, or bear the mark of Ch'êng Hua. The subjects of decoration are sages in landscapes, flowering plants, phoenixes, or more rarely tigers or horses in landscapes. The dishes are coarsely made, with roughly finished foot rims and with radial 'chatter marks' on the base, and sometimes with coarse grit adhering to it. These dishes are greatly

[1] Jenyns, *Later Chinese Porcelain*, takes the Transition Period to extend to 1683 and there is something to be said for this point of view. But the Imperial potteries of K'ang Hsi were active many years before this and were producing some porcelain not very different from that made after 1683. I have preferred, therefore, to take the earlier date for the end of the Transition Period.

prized in Japan, and are far better represented in Japanese than in western collections.[1] Much better in quality are an alms bowl (1) with an inscription saying that it was made in the first year of T'ien Ch'i (1621) and an incense burner,[2] with a cyclical mark corresponding to 1626. Another T'ien Ch'i piece is an incense burner decorated with three-clawed dragons and with a long inscription dated 1625, stating that it was made for the venerable gentleman Min Yang, in the Ho-nei department of the Huai-Ch'ing prefectural district in the province of Honan.[3] A similar piece, made for the same venerable gentleman, is dated thirteen years earlier, in the thirty-ninth year of Wan Li (A.D. 1612).[4] Both these pieces, as is usual with presentation wares, are rather coarsely made.

Still fewer pieces are known with the mark of Ch'ung Chêng. One of these is a coarsely made dish with foliated edge decorated with a three-clawed dragon affronté and inscribed with the first year of the reign (1628) (2). A third incense burner, similar to the two just mentioned, made for the same prefectural district Huai-Ch'ing and dated 1632,[5] and a few small cups bearing the Ch'ung Chêng mark[6] seem to complete the marked blue and white of the period, except for a few vases of a special type to which reference will be made later.

We saw that there is evidence that, in spite of the decline in quality that occurred in the Wan Li period, a reasonably high standard of potting and decoration was maintained in the Imperial potteries right to the end of Wan Li's reign. The marked pieces of the T'ien Ch'i and Ch'ung Chêng periods just described do not approach in quality even the poorer Wan Li pieces and we must conclude that either the Imperial potteries closed down or else that they reached a very low ebb indeed after the death of Wan Li.

The real ceramic interest in this period lies in the so-called 'Transition Wares', which seem to have been made from the time of T'ien Ch'i to the early days of K'ang Hsi. Attention was first drawn to the importance of these wares by Perzynski.[7] It is difficult to date them exactly because no examples are known with a seventeenth century reign mark, although they occasionally bear the mark of Chia Ching. There are, however, three pieces with cyclical date marks that can be

[1] See *Old Oriental Ceramics Donated by Mr. Yokogawa*, Tokyo National Museum, 1953.
[2] Jenyns, *loc. cit.*, Plate I, 1B.
[3] [4] Jenyns, *Ming Pottery and Porcelain*, Plates 108A, 108B.
[5] *O.C.S. Trans.*, 1926–27, Plate II, Figs. 2, 3.
[6] Jenyns, *Later Chinese Porcelain*, Plate II, 1C.
[7] *Burlington Magazine*, 1910–11.

(1) *Plate* 59A; (2) *Plate* 59B.

accepted as belonging to the fourth decade of the seventeenth century. These are a blue and white vase (1) belonging to Mr. Gerald Reitlinger, a blue and white vase belonging to Mr. Richard de la Mare that has been covered by a green glaze on a second firing,[1] and a blue and white vase at Chantilly. These bear dates corresponding to 1636, 1638 and 1639 respectively.[2] A number of other pieces have been fitted with datable European mounts. The designs on Transition Wares were extensively copied in European delft ware during the latter half of the seventeenth century.

The Transition Wares vary in quality but the best of them, consisting almost entirely of vases, reach a very high standard. The paste and glaze are of fine quality and the blue, with a slight purplish tint generally less strong than the typical Chia Ching blue, is very attractive. The colour has been described as resembling 'violets in milk'. The bases of the vases are often unglazed, revealing the fine texture of the paste. The decoration is almost always of landscapes, with or without human figures (2), or of groups of growing plants (3). An occasional piece is found decorated in more formal style (4). The vases are often decorated in addition with one or more delicately incised narrow bands of flower scrolls or waves.[3]

The Transition Wares introduced a new style of painting into ceramic art, less formal than that adopted in the Imperial sixteenth century wares in which the landscape usually served as a background to the human figures. The Transition Wares seem to be a natural development of the sixteenth century non-Imperial wares which, as we have seen, broke away from the Imperial styles. But the precipitous mountains and waterfalls surrounded by swirling clouds (5) and the sensitively drawn growing plants (6) show a new appreciation of natural beauty, as might be expected in an age that saw a great revival in landscape painting.[4]

The style of painting, although continued into the K'ang Hsi period, enables Transition Wares to be easily identified. The shapes of the vases sometimes show European influence and many of them are decorated with formal tulip-like flowers which may be the result of the same influence (7). The floral sprays dividing the landscape

[1] Honey, *Ceramic Art of China*, Plate 99.
[2] See Chapter 12 for further information on cyclical marks.
[3] The vases in Plates 60B, 61A, 61B are so decorated. The decoration is visible in Plate 60B.
[4] See J. P. Dubosc, 'A New Approach to Chinese Painting,' *Oriental Art*, 1950, Vol. III, No. 2.

(1) *Plate* 60B; (2) *Plates* 60A, 60C; (3) *Plates* 61A, 61B; (4) *Plate* 63A; (5) *Plate* 60C; (6) *Plates* 61A. 61B; (7) *Plate* 63A.

F. MID-SEVENTEENTH CENTURY. HT. 16.5 in.
Mr. Max Robertson
See page xxiii

panels in the bowl (1) are also European in origin. There are certain details of technique, such as the method of drawing grass by a series of V-shaped strokes, which help in identification. This particular technique has been unfavourably commented on by some ceramics writers, but similar mannerisms are part of the stock in trade of ceramic artists and can be found in all periods of blue and white, from the fourteenth century onwards.

This was the period of the development of the story in pictures which became very popular in the K'ang Hsi period. Fairy tales, stories of popular heroes and beautiful maidens abound. The device of representing a dream by a separate enclosed picture, a feature of modern comic cartoons, is also used. The vase illustrated in Plate 62 shows a civil servant who has dined too well and has fallen asleep at his desk. On the other side of the vase is depicted his dream, in which he is shown bursting into the garden of his ladylove by moonlight.

The sudden appearance of these beautiful wares during the first half of the seventeenth century may perhaps be explained by the absence of work for the potters at the Imperial kilns, who then set up potteries where they were able to develop their ideas free from the restrictive control of the Court.

Some time has been devoted to the Transition wares firstly because of their intrinsic qualities, secondly because they mark a change of style which had a pronounced influence on later wares and thirdly because many of the fine copies of pieces of earlier Ming reigns may well have been made by the Transition potters. Jenyns has suggested[1] that a fine small polychrome box and cover, formerly in the Oppenheim collection, with the Ch'êng Hua mark and long accepted as belonging to the period, is a transition piece. The group of small pieces shown in Plate 65A may also belong to this period.

The seventeenth-century potters were also very successful in imitating the Chia Ching blue and white. Striking confirmation of this is provided by a dated dish in the David Foundation, (2) which was made for Hung Kuang, the grandson of Wan Li, who attempted to seize power in 1644, but was defeated and killed in 1645. This dish, made in 1645,[2] is decorated in a dark purplish blue similar to that used in Imperial Chia Ching pieces and it might very well, if unmarked, be placed in the sixteenth century. Indeed, there is a

---

[1] Jenyns, *Later Chinese Porcelain*, p. 19.

[2] There is a blue and white bottle in the British Museum (see Jenyns, *Ming Pottery and Porcelain*, Plate 110B), marked *Fu fan chih tsao*, which is now interpreted 'Made for the Prince of Fu'. This was one of the titles of Hung Kuang, and the piece was probably made either for him or his father Chu Ch'ung-Hsu.

---

(1) *Plate* 63B; (2) *Plate* 64A.

group of blue and white dishes, generally with a brown edge and bearing the Chia Ching mark, which have until recently been accepted as of the period.[1] A group of these dishes is shown in Plate 65B. Two of them, with the Chia Ching mark, are probably early K'ang Hsi, while the third, with the Ch'êng Hua mark, belongs to the first half of the seventeenth century.

Because large numbers of the Transition Wares were exported to Europe, and because some of them have European shapes and bear border designs of Western origin, some writers have concluded that they were made entirely for export. But the main subjects of design are purely Chinese and must have appealed strongly to Chinese taste. Indeed, it seems most unlikely that over a period of forty years a group of porcelain far superior to the rest should have been made for export only. As for the European designs, the whole history of Chinese porcelain shows how readily foreign ideas were absorbed and made to fit into the Chinese pattern.

[1] Cf. *Philadelphia Museum Bulletin*, No. 223, Plate No. 113.

7

THE REIGN OF K'ANG HSI

We have seen how the export of blue and white grew steadily during the Ming dynasty. By the beginning of the seventeenth century large quantities were being exported to Europe and were greatly influencing European ceramic art. The export wares of the Ming dynasty, although generally Chinese in taste and only different in refinement from the better wares made for Chinese use, are quite different from those made in the Imperial potteries for the use of the Court which were, of course, not exported. It was not until the third decade of the twentieth century that the west became familiar with the Imperial blue and white, generally of far higher quality than the export wares.

The breakdown of the Ming dynasty liberated ceramics from the control of the Court and, as we have seen, the finest blue and white of the seventeenth century was not made to Imperial order, but in private factories for general use. The Transition Wares, in spite of the European influence that some of them show, were not specially made for export, although they were freely available for this purpose. Thus, for the first time, examples of the best Chinese blue and white of its day began to appear in Europe.

As the Ch'ing dynasty became firmly established the control of the best ceramic wares by the Imperial Court began to be resumed but, if we may judge by the quality of the pieces exported right up to the end of the seventeenth century, it was not until the eighteenth century that a clear distinction between pieces made for Imperial use and those made for private individuals began to be established once more. The impact of these non-Imperial wares, particularly those of the second half of the seventeenth century, on Europe was tremendous. For two centuries they were regarded as the summit of achievement of blue and white. This is not surprising. The K'ang Hsi blue and white reached a technical excellence that has never been surpassed. The porcelain, pure white and of fine texture, is covered with a glaze of slightly bluish or greenish tint and the decoration, at its best, is in a pure blue of great luminosity. Although the European potters were never able to approach the quality of Chinese blue and white, some of the copies of Chinese blue and white in delftware are surprisingly good, in view of the differences of material.

The interest in Europe for K'ang Hsi blue and white waned during the second half of the eighteenth and nineteenth centuries, when the brightly coloured Chinese *famille verte* and *famille rose* and the Japanese Kakiemon porcelain were the most popular oriental types. There was a revival of interest in blue and white in the mid-nineteenth century led by a small group that included Whistler, Rossetti and other artists. The catalogue of one collection of this period, that of Henry Thompson, was actually illustrated by engravings mainly drawn by Whistler.[1] The recent re-awakening in interest in blue and white has been confined mainly to the fourteenth and fifteenth century wares. But the qualities that made K'ang Hsi blue and white so attractive to the artists and connoisseurs of the nineteenth century remain, and it will surely come back to its own once more.

*   *   *   *   *   *   *

Before we deal in detail with the reign of K'ang Hsi, some reference should be made to the first reign of the Ch'ing dynasty, that of Shun Chih (1644–1661). There are few marked pieces of this reign. The best known are a number of dishes, incised with five-clawed dragons under a blue glaze, which bear the six-character mark of Shun Chih, probably made for Imperial use. A blue and white incense burner, dated 1655 (1), in the David Foundation, was made for presentation and follows the usual pattern of such pieces. It should be compared with the earlier examples already discussed[2] and later examples belonging to the reign of K'ang Hsi.[3] Another blue and white piece of this reign, bearing the four-character mark, is a smaller incense burner, decorated with plum blossoms and bamboo leaves on a background of cracked ice,[4] the fore-runner of a type of decoration that was to become very popular in the next reign. There can be no doubt that Transition Wares and pieces in Chia Ching style continued to be made throughout this reign.

The first twenty years or so of the reign of K'ang Hsi (1662–1722) were somewhat unsettled and it was not until 1683, when Ts'ang

---

[1] *Catalogue of Blue and White Nankin Porcelain from the Collection of Henry Thompson, with Autotypes after Drawings by Whistler and Thompson*, London 1878.

[2] See p. 39.

[3] Jenyns, *Later Chinese Porcelain*, Plates VIII, XII.

[4] *Chinese Blue and White Exhibition*, 1953–54, No. 230 (Plate 15A).

(1) *Plate* 64B.

G. T'IEN-CH'I PERIOD. DIAM. 6.2 in.
See page xxiv

Ying-hsüan was made Director of the Imperial factory that it settled down, under Imperial patronage, to produce the fine wares characteristic of the K'ang Hsi period. An account of the vicissitudes of the early period has been given by Jenyns,[1] who indeed has included it as part of the Transition period, but in fact this early period saw the introduction of new types, some of which bear the mark of K'ang Hsi.

Two early examples of the K'ang Hsi period are shown in Plate 66. The first (1) shows a survival of a Ming style of drawing. Without its four-character mark of K'ang Hsi it might well be placed in the first half of the seventeenth century. The second (2) belongs to a class already referred to,[2] generally bearing the Chia Ching mark, but in this instance correctly marked. There are a number of dishes of good quality, rather heavily built and fitted with a deep semi-circular groove underneath, which also belong to the period before 1683. Several dishes of this type, with some copper red decoration added to the blue, actually bear the cyclical date corresponding to 1672.[3] The blue and white dishes are sometimes correctly marked, sometimes bear the Ch'êng Hua mark and sometimes an emblem such as an artemisia leaf. The dish in Plate 67 is unmarked. The decoration, of galloping horses on a wave background, is another Ming survival. The pattern is frequently found in seventeenth-century pieces decorated on the biscuit. The calligraphy of this period is in a bold style, quite distinct from that of the later part of K'ang Hsi's reign.[4]

The period from 1683 onwards is that during which the typical K'ang Hsi blue and white, which aroused so much interest in Europe in the eighteenth and nineteenth centuries, was made. We know a good deal about the methods of manufacture from the two famous letters of Père d'Entrecolles of 1712 and 1722.[5] We are told that methods of mass production were used, and that a single piece could pass through as many as seventy hands before it was ready for firing. Under these conditions we must expect a lack of spontaneity in the decoration. But although the drawing of many pieces is perfunctory, we can find plenty of examples with real artistic merit, which must have been decorated, in the main, by a single artist. We shall refer to some of these later.

[1] *Later Chinese Porcelain*, pp. 17–27.
[2] See pp. 41, 42.
[3] Jenyns, *loc. cit.*, Plate XVIII.
[4] Mention should be made of five cups dated 1665, 1666, 1666, 1668 and 1669 respectively, belonging to Mr. Riesco, exhibited in the *O.C.S. Exhibition of Blue and White*, 1953–54 (Nos. 231–235).
[5] Bushell, *Translation of the T'ao Shuo*, 1910.

(1) *Plate* 66A; (2) *Plate* 66B.

ORIENTAL BLUE AND WHITE

Only a small proportion of the pieces of this period bear the mark of K'ang Hsi, a fact that led, in the minds of past connoisseurs, to much confusion, which was only dispelled in the twentieth century. Chang Ch'i-ching, the superintendent of the Imperial factories between 1677 and 1680, issued an edict forbidding the potters to use the *nien hao* of the Emperor on their pots. We have no direct evidence as to how strictly this law was kept or whether it was ever officially withdrawn, but the relatively small number of correctly marked pieces suggests that the order must have been partially effective. A large number of pieces bear the marks of Ming Emperors, particularly that of Ch'êng Hua and, to a less extent, that of Hsüan Tê, and the practice of using a symbol, such as an artemisia leaf, an incense burner or a lotus blossom, generally enclosed in a double ring, which had been only sparingly in use during the Ming dynasty, became common. Sometimes the double ring alone was used.

It should be possible, by systematic study of the wealth of material available from this period, to place the different groups in some sort of order. Perzynski started a study of this kind but did not get very far.[1] At present therefore we must rely on conjecture in making any attempt at exact dating. A plate (1) commemorating riots in Rotterdam in 1690, and therefore likely to have been made before the end of the seventeenth century, is decorated, except for the central theme, entirely in Chinese style and has the Ch'êng Hua mark. It is typical of many K'ang Hsi pieces and enables us to place them as belonging to the end of the seventeenth century. The dish in Colour Plate K, which has the correct mark of the period, and the pair of dishes (2), with the more usual mark of Ch'êng Hua, are fine examples of this class. The bottle with a picture of a man and woman hunting a hare (3), which for some reason is generally described as a 'love chase', and the oviform vase with mountains and waterfalls (4) are examples of K'ang Hsi blue and white at its most glowing, while the bowl (5) reproduces skilfully, with its washes of pale blue, the effect of a snowy landscape. But the glory of K'ang Hsi blue and white is perhaps best revealed by the large vases in the great museums of the west. The two examples from the Victoria and Albert Museum illustrate, on the one hand (6) a vase of typical K'ang Hsi shape decorated with the familiar theme of a landscape of pine trees, storks and deer, the usual emblems of immortality, while the other, a bottle (7), shows great skill in a plum blossom design reserved on a blue ground. This style of decoration is

[1] *Burlington Magazine*, 1910–11.

---

(1) *Plate* 68; (2) *Plate* 72; (3) *Plate* 69A; (4) *Plate* 69B; (5) *Plate* 69C; (6) *Plate* 70; (7) *Plate* 71.

more usually found on the so-called 'ginger jars',[1] one of the most popular forms of blue and white, which has been copied extensively right up to the present day. The pair of saucer dishes (1), with their sensitive drawing of cranes and peach trees, surely refute the argument, often put forward, that the drawing on K'ang Hsi blue and white is always mechanical.

Towards the end of the reign of K'ang Hsi there was a trend towards closer Imperial control of the best class of porcelain. This is illustrated by the 'birthday plates'[2] and the small pieces made in peach bloom and other monochrome glazes.[3] The bottle (2) and brush pot (3) probably belong to this late period. They both bear the K'ang Hsi mark, in characteristically neat calligraphy, very different from that of the earlier K'ang Hsi wares.

[1] Honey, *Guide to Later Chinese Porcelain*, Plate 21.
[2] Jenyns, *Later Chinese Porcelain*, Plate XXIX.
[3] Honey, *loc. cit.*, Plates 7A, 13A.

(1) *Plate 73*; (2) *Plate 74A*; (3) *Plate 74B*.

8

YUNG CHÊNG AND SUBSEQUENT
REIGNS OF THE CH'ING DYNASTY

We saw that towards the end of the reign of K'ang Hsi there was a trend for the manufacture of fine porcelain to come more under Imperial control. This trend became stronger in the reign of his successor, Yung Chêng (1723–1735). This was a period of active experimentation, not only in the production of new glazes, but also in copying, as closely as possible, the classical Sung and Ming wares. According to the T'ao Lu,[1] 'reproductions of the old and new inventions can really be said to stem from this period.'

A list, compiled by T'ang Ying, sometime between 1729 and 1732,[2] which describes a number of different types of porcelain required by the Court, gives us some idea, however incomplete, of the variety of the wares made in the reign of Yung Chêng. T'ang Ying, who has the reputation of being the most skilful potter of the eighteenth century,[3] was at this time assistant to Nien Hsi-yao, the Superintendent of the Imperial factories. T'ang Ying succeeded Nien Hsi-yao in 1736 and held the post of Superintendent until 1749. There are only three types of blue and white in his list, out of a total of nearly sixty. These are copies of Hsüan Tê,[4] Ch'êng Hua and Chia Ching. Fortunately many of the copies are correctly marked, so that those with the mark of the period imitated can generally be correctly ascribed.[5] In copying the blue and white of the Hsüan Tê period the potters attempted to simulate the 'heaped and piled' decoration, and they also added dots to the outlines to imitate those found in the earlier wares. As a rule these attempts are not good enough to deceive anyone

---

[1] *Ching-tê Chên T'ao Lu*, translated by Geoffrey R. Sayer.

[2] *Loc. cit.*, p. 22. See also Honey, *Guide to Later Chinese Porcelain*, p. 74.

[3] A full account of T'ang Ying is given in Jenyns, *Later Chinese Porcelain*.

[4] The reference to the Hsüan Tê copies is vague. The type is generally taken to be blue and white, but it may be porcelain covered with a plain blue glaze.

[5] It is an interesting point that the copies of Hsüan Tê generally bear the Yung Chêng or Ch'ien Lung mark in seal characters while those of Ch'êng Hua are marked in ordinary script. The use of seal characters, which first became common during the Yung Chêng period, continued throughout the Ch'ing dynasty.

familiar with the originals, although there are a few exceptions. Good examples are shown in Plates 75, 76. In the former the artist, in the freely drawn flower sprays, has made a very good imitation of the fifteenth-century style of painting, but the texture of the glaze and the absence of the 'heaped and piled' effect would proclaim its eighteenth-century origin, even if we had not the Yung Chêng mark to settle the matter. The large vase in Plate 76 with a shape copied from a vase of the T'ang period, is too neat and tidy and the drawing too mechanical for it to belong to the earlier period. The perfume holder with the Ch'ien Lung mark (I) is a later piece in the style of the fifteenth century. It probably belongs to the later part of the reign. It bears, in addition to the reign mark, the mark of the potter who made the piece, Chin Ting-ch'êng.

The copies of Ch'êng Hua blue and white are more skilful than those of Hsüan Tê, no doubt because the more delicate style of painting and the thinner and more transparent glaze of Ch'êng Hua porcelain conformed more closely to the standards of the eighteenth century potters than did the heavier style and thicker glaze of Hsüan Tê. Two good copies, both correctly marked, have already been seen, with the originals, in Plates 36, 37. When the copies and the originals are examined side by side the subtle differences that distinguish them can be seen. But there are many pieces with the earlier mark that present great difficulties in identification, even to experts. The difficulties are accentuated when the pieces are small, so that differences in the technique of manufacture are difficult to distinguish. A number of small cups, some in blue and white alone, and some with the addition of *tou ts'ai* enamels, in this category are illustrated in Jenyns's *Later Chinese Porcelain*.[1]

The Yung Chêng copies of blue and white, as well as of many other types of Sung and Ming porcelain, are probably the most skilful in the whole field of Chinese ceramics. Brankston[2] refers to the excellence of copies with the K'ang Hsi mark, but no examples of such copies in blue and white seem to be represented in Western collections. Some pieces in Ch'êng Hua style with the K'ang Hsi mark are certainly known. But they are not particularly good copies and some of them are not even of the K'ang Hsi period.

Apart from the copies of earlier wares, blue and white in the K'ang Hsi tradition continued to be made. But the interest at this time was more in the great variety of new monochrome glazes made possible by

[1] Plate XXIV.
[2] *Early Ming Wares of Ching-tê Chên*, p. 43.

(I) *Plate 77.*

the introduction of new pigments and in the brightly coloured *famille rose*. Two good examples of marked Yung Chêng blue and white, well up to K'ang Hsi standards, are shown in Plate 78. The stem cup, with its broad ribbed stem, is of a shape found in a number of Imperial pieces, with glazes from the high-fired copper red to green and yellow enamels.[1] The decoration on the blue and white stem cup, although resembling somewhat the Ch'êng Hua style, is not sufficiently close to be regarded as a copy. The subject of decoration of the bowl, the Eight Immortals on waves, is one that appears on pieces in the succeeding reigns Ch'ien Lung (1736–1795) and Chia Ch'ing (1796–1820). The standard of blue and white was steadily deteriorating during these two reigns, but occasional pieces of fair quality were still made (1).

In addition to such pieces, made for the Chinese, large quantities of blue and white were made for export. This varied greatly in quality, but even the best was much inferior to the earlier K'ang Hsi blue and white. Generally described as 'Old Nankin China', it was treasured in the homes of wealthy and middle-class families in Europe, and inspired the decoration of European porcelain and earthenware. Typical examples of export blue and white (2), belonging to the second half of the eighteenth century, show borders and other features that indicate European influence. For the first time the designs on Chinese porcelain were made to meet the requirements of European customers in every detail. Patterns of borders and designs, armorial shields and European engravings were copied accurately,[2] in so far as European culture could be understood by the Chinese potters.

*   *   *   *   *   *   *

One innovation generally associated with the reign of Ch'ien Lung, although actually started in the K'ang Hsi period, is what is known as 'soft paste' blue and white. According to Père d'Entrecolles in his second letter, the technique was new in 1722. He describes soft paste as rare, much dearer than the ordinary porcelain, and compares it, as a medium for painting, with the ordinary porcelain as vellum is to paper. His enthusiastic views are not entirely supported by the T'ao Lu, which describes the material as excellent, but says that the glaze is not so brilliant as that of the hard paste. It goes on to say that soft paste was not much used for 'official old' ware, the porcelain of the first quality.

[1] See Jenyns, *Later Chinese Porcelain*, Plate XXXVI, 2.
[2] Honey, *Guide to Later Chinese Porcelain*, Plates 110, 112.

(1) *Plates* 79A, 79B; (2) *Plates* 80A, 80B, 82A.

H. SHONZUI WARE, CH'UNG-CHÊNG PERIOD. HT. 7.1 in.
Japanese Collection
See pages xxv, xxvi

YUNG CHÊNG AND SUBSEQUENT REIGNS

A good deal of misunderstanding has arisen on the materials used in the manufacture of Chinese soft paste because Père d'Entrecolles described the body material as *hua-shih* (slippery stone), a description that led European potters in the eighteenth century to think that the material was soapstone or steatite. Indeed this led to the manufacture of steatitic porcelain at Bristol and Worcester after 1749.

A good deal of work was done on the analysis of samples of Chinese materials by Ebelman and Salvétat in 1850[1] and Vogt in 1900.[2] The work is inconclusive because there is evidence of changes in the materials used for the manufacture of porcelain in China during the nineteenth century and the work thus provides no evidence on the materials of the eighteenth century. Such limited analyses as have been made of eighteenth century soft paste suggest that the material used was not very different from that of hard paste porcelain, but that the temperature of firing was lower, so that the body was not completely vitrified, while the absence of magnesium shows that steatite was not used. More analyses, however, are necessary before we can say with certainty that steatite was never used in soft paste.[3]

An examination of actual pieces of soft paste porcelain shows that they are made of a hard opaque material—and thus are not porcelain at all by the usual Western standards[4]—covered with a glaze which is creamy in tint and sometimes crackled, and painted in a distinctive style with delicate brushwork (1). The blue is not so bright as in the hard paste porcelain, possibly the result of the firing being at a lower temperature. The cream-coloured background, very different from the bluish or greenish tint of hard paste, suggests that an oxidising atmosphere was used in the firing. The pieces of soft paste are generally small and thinly potted. The thinness of the potting has led, incorrectly, to the view that the material itself is light. Soft paste was used extensively in the manufacture of snuff bottles and other miniature objects, which was started in the eighteenth century, and continued throughout the nineteenth century.

*   *   *   *   *   *   *

The decline in standards, started in the reign of Ch'ien Lung, continued rapidly in the subsequent reigns of the Ch'ing dynasty, Chia

[1] *Annales de Chimie et de Physique*, Tome 31, 1851.
[2] *Bulletin de la Société d'encouragement pour l'industrie nationale*, April 1900.
[3] Ebelman and Salvétat suggest that *hua-shih* was generally used for slip decoration.
[4] See Rosenthal, *Pottery and Ceramics.*

(1) *Plates* 81A, 81B.

Ch'ing (1796–1820), Tao Kuang (1821–1850), Hsien Feng (1851–1861), T'ung Chih (1862–1874) and Kuang Hsü (1875–1908). The decline is particularly noticeable in the quality of the porcelain itself and the white glaze. The clear smooth slightly greenish glaze of the early eighteenth century was replaced by a glaze of poor colour, often greyish, with a slightly uneven surface of the type described as 'orange peel'. For the majority of the nineteenth-century wares, in which most of the surface was covered with heavily brocaded coloured patterns, the deterioration was not vital. But it could not be hidden when underglaze blue decoration was used, and it is not surprising that the popularity of blue and white, now so obviously inferior to the earlier wares, declined.

In the Chia Ch'ing and Tao Kuang periods some of the best blue and white is to be found in the interior of the so-called 'Pekin bowls', decorated outside in *famille rose* enamels on grounds of yellow, blue or rose enriched with scroll decorations in other colours. A late eighteenth-century piece of Chia Ch'ing blue and white, dated 1798 (1), and decorated in European style, has been further embellished by having had the body pierced with a perforated design before the glaze was applied. This type of decoration, sometimes known as 'rice-grain', which is found in Persian pottery as early as the twelfth century, seems to have first appeared on Chinese porcelain in the Ch'ien Lung period. Three examples of the Tao Kuang (2), T'ung Chih (3) and Kuang Hsü (4) periods are typical of Imperial work, and illustrate the steady decline in quality during the nineteenth century. In the last period, Kuang Hsü, a number of copies of earlier wares were made, and in particular copies of the dishes decorated with the three friends, of which Hsüan Tê and Ch'êng Hua examples were seen in Plates 32A, 32B and which were also made in the earlier Ch'ing reigns.[1] The Kuang Hsü copies have little to recommend them but, as the last of a series of dishes to the same design which cover a period of nearly five hundred years, they serve as a striking example of the strength of Chinese tradition.

Something should be said about the Chinese blue and white of the twentieth century. Porcelain of far higher quality than anything produced in the nineteenth century, devoted entirely to copies of the earlier Ming and Ch'ing wares, has been made in China in recent years and particularly in the third and fourth decades of this century. These are fakes in the true sense, and the Chinese connoisseur will

---

[1] *O.C.S. Chinese Blue and White Exhibition*, 1953–54, London, 1953–54. Nos. 305, 313, 318, 320, 321.

(1) *Plate* 82A; (2) *Plate* 82B; (3) *Plate* 83A; (4) *Plate* 83B.

need to use all his resources, both artistic and technical, to detect them. But the outlook of the craftsmen who made the pieces and the conditions of manufacture are so different, in the genuine wares and the copies, that it is only a matter of time before they all appear in the right perspective.

9

PROVINCIAL CHINESE
BLUE AND WHITE

Although Ching-tê Chên and its neighbourhood in Kiangsi was the home of blue and white and continued as the centre of manufacture throughout the Ming and Ch'ing dynasties, a good deal of blue and white was made at other places in China. Our knowledge about these provincial wares is very sketchy, but we do know a little about two large groups, one made in the southern province of Annam,[1] and another in Fukien, a province bordering Kiangsi. The latter are generally known as Swatow wares, because they were once thought to have been exported from this port to Japan, the Philippines and the islands of the East Indian Archipelago.

*   *   *   *   *   *   *

The manufacture of Annamese blue and white was in full swing during the fifteenth century, but we have no evidence at present as to when it actually started. An important documentary piece in the Serai at Istanbul (1) bears an inscription stating that it was painted by a workman of Nan Ts'e-chou in the eighth year of Ta Ho. Nan Ts'e-chou is in Annam and Ta (or T'ai) Ho reigned in Annam from 1443 to 1454. This gives the date of manufacture as 1450. The decoration of this piece, while based on motives found on Imperial porcelain of the fifteenth century, has a number of clearly defined qualities, such as the linear style of drawing in the border designs, and we have no difficulty in finding other pieces that belong to the same group. These include a squat globular jar (2) and a fine oviform jar (3) said to have come from the Yemen. The latter, painted more freely than the other two pieces illustrated, shows a close resemblance, particularly in the flower scroll that forms the main band of decoration, to fourteenth-century blue and white. It may well be earlier than the dated bottle, possibly belonging to the beginning of the fifteenth century. The

[1] The evidence that these wares were made in Annam is circumstantial. No blue and white kiln sites have yet been discovered in Annam.

(1) *Plate* 84A; (2) *Plate* 84B; (3) *Plate* 85.

formal flower sprays that appear on the shoulders of this jar and other motives may be found, in simplified form, on a number of small jars which may also be presumed to be Annamese.[1] The bases of the pieces, which are usually cleanly finished, unlike those of Swatow which generally have large accretions of sand on the glazed bases, are unglazed, but are often covered with a brown wash.

It seems likely that the manufacture of blue and white in Annam continued throughout the Ming dynasty, if not longer, but we have as yet no means of distinguishing the earlier and later pieces. The dish (1), with its freely drawn central subject of birds on prunus branches, shows a departure from the more formal styles already noted and may belong to the sixteenth rather than the fifteenth century.

The Annamese wares were exported in large numbers to the Archipelago, but not generally to the West. They are not therefore well represented in the West, except in such collections as that of the Princessehof Museum in Leeuwarden, which has been built up on pieces found in the Dutch East Indies.

*   *   *   *   *   *   *

The so-called Swatow wares consist of coarsely-made dishes (2) and jars with loop handles on the shoulders (3), decorated either in blue and white or in green, turquoise and red enamels. They have been found in large numbers in the Philippines and the East Indian Archipelago, as well as in Japan, where they are very highly prized. The blue and white wares, which concern us here, are freely and sometimes crudely decorated with such subjects as dragons, which are often curiously provided with four spindly legs,[2] phoenixes, or birds on flowering branches (4). The paint generally seems to have been applied with a wet brush, leaving blobs of colour where the brush strokes end.

We have no definite information as to where and when these pieces were made, but they almost certainly belong to the province of Fukien. They may have been made at Ch'ao Chou, where potteries existed in the Sung dynasty and within two miles of which, at

[1] Honey, *The Ceramic Art of China*, Plate 147.

[2] Jars with this decoration are illustrated in Nanne Ottema, *Chineesche ceramik, handboek geschreven naar aanleiding van de verzamelingen in het Museum het Princessehof te Leeuwarden*, Amsterdam, 1946. See also John A. Pope, 'The Princessehof Museum in Leeuwarden,' *Archives, Chinese Art Society of America*, 1951.

(1) *Plate* 86A; (2) *Plates* 86B, 88B; (3) *Plate* 87; (4) *Plate* 88A.

Funkai, coarse pottery is being made today.[1] On grounds of style the
Swatow wares may be attributed to the Ming dynasty, not earlier
than the middle of the sixteenth century. The Portuguese records of
the mid-sixteenth century make a distinction between fine and coarse
porcelain and the Swatow wares may well have been included in the
latter class; but coarse porcelain was also, of course, being made at
Ching-tê Chên, as well as the finer wares.

There seems to be no justification for the use of the term 'Swatow'
in describing these wares. Swatow was of no importance until it
became a treaty port in 1860 and it seems to be unrecorded in maps of
the Ming period.[2] However, like many other descriptive terms in
Chinese porcelain, the term has become established and it seems
desirable not to cause further confusion by abandoning it.

Another group of blue and white made in the province of Fukien
is represented by dishes with flat unglazed bases and 'baking pan'
sides (I), decorated with brushwork not unlike that of the Swatow
wares. But the material of the body of these dishes and the finish of
the bases is much finer. Indeed, the material of the body resembles
closely that of the white 'blanc de chine' wares of Tê-hua and they
may be tentatively ascribed to the Tê-hua potteries.

*   *   *   *   *   *   *

There are other groups of blue and white, different from any of
those already discussed, about which little is known at present. One
of these consists of dishes with bases sometimes glazed and sometimes
unglazed and deeply undercut foot rims. They are generally decorated
in fifteenth-century style,[3] but they probably date from the early
sixteenth century onwards. Although heavily constructed, the dishes
are made of fine materials and are well finished. They are generally
found in the Archipelago and other places where Annamese and
Swatow wares are found, but they have little resemblance to either
of these wares, nor to the normal export wares of Ching-tê chên.
They may have been made at some as yet unidentified site in
Southern China.

A second group consists of dishes decorated with coarse chrysanthemums scrolls with a background of scrawls which appear to be roughly

[1] 'Symposium on Ch'ao Chou Wares,' T. Volker, J. M. Plumer and others, *Far
Eastern Ceramic Bulletin*, June 1953.

[2] *Loc. cit.*

[3] A number of dishes of this type are in the Leeuwarden Museum.

(I) *Plates* 89A, 89B.

drawn Arabic characters.[1] The provenance of this type is uncertain, although it may very well have been made in the neighbourhood of Ching-tê chên. The earlier pieces seem to have been made in the seventeenth century, but the type persisted through the eighteenth century up to the nineteenth. Indeed similarly made dishes, decorated in blue with an occasional detail in copper red, were being made in China in recent times.

[1] Kamer Aga-Oglu, 'Blue and White Porcelain Plates made for Moslem Patrons,' *Far Eastern Ceramic Bulletin*, September 1951.

10

KOREAN BLUE AND WHITE

The manufacture of blue and white in Korea took place at a late stage in the country's ceramic history, probably not before the beginning of the seventeenth century. The most important wares of the Koryu dynasty (918–1392) were celadon wares, either undecorated or decorated in simple incised or inlaid designs. Painted wares with bold brushwork in a brown pigment were also produced towards the end of this period. The Koryu dynasty was succeeded by the Yi dynasty (1392–1910), during which some of the earlier types continued to be made. At the end of the sixteenth century Korea was over-run and ravaged by the Japanese, and after this disaster the rulers of the country succeeded in isolating it almost entirely from the outside world. The 'Hermit Country', as it was called, continued in a state of extreme poverty right up to the twentieth century.

It is not surprising that the blue and white, which was all made during this period of poverty, is not of the same technical quality as the earlier Korean wares or the contemporary Chinese ones. The body of the wares is a rather coarse greyish-white porcelain. The pieces are roughly finished and are often found with coarse sand, on which the pieces stood during firing, adhering to the glazed base. The decoration, generally of dragons or simple flower sprays, is painted in a greyish blue. The best known pieces, and possibly the earliest, are the dragon jars (1) which were made in various sizes, some of them being very large. The drawing, which follows the style of earlier pieces painted in brown on a coarse grey stoneware, is full of vigour.

Another group of Korean blue and white wares consists of small jars and bowls (2), which are better in material and finish than the dragon jars. The designs, tamer and more sophisticated than those of the pieces already referred to, are not without charm, which is enhanced by the soft matt appearance of the glaze. In the absence of any direct evidence on the dating of these pieces, we may tentatively place them as belonging to a period starting at the beginning of the

(1) *Plate* 90; (2) *Plates* 91A, 91B.

eighteenth century and possibly going on to the nineteenth century. Although the designs are quite distinctive, they seem to owe something to Japanese influence and it is possible that, in spite of the isolation of Korea, foreign ideas slowly infiltrated and influenced the country's ceramic art.

11

JAPANESE BLUE AND WHITE

Although our knowledge of Chinese blue and white leaves a good deal to be desired, we have some satisfaction in knowing that it has grown greatly during the last twenty years and is still being extended. Unfortunately we cannot say the same about Japanese blue and white. Hobson's contribution to the subject in 1924[1] showed how little was known about it then, and it is true to say that there has been little addition to our knowledge since. This is partly because of the small amount of interest in Japanese porcelain in the West and partly because little attention has been devoted so far in Japan to the question of determining the exact provenance of the various types of Japanese porcelain.

The historical facts, if this description can be used about events that are almost legendary, are that porcelain was first made in Japan by Gorodayu go Shonzui. He is said to have gone to Ching-tê Chên in 1510 and to have stayed there for five years, before going back, with a supply of Chinese materials, to make blue and white porcelain in Japan. He settled in Arita, in the province of Hizen, and made porcelain until his stock of materials was exhausted. He failed to find suitable materials in Japan, although they were available a few miles away from Arita.

The evidence about the first manufacture of porcelain in Japan from local materials is a little more substantial. The deposits of porcelain stone were discovered at Izumiyama, close to Arita, by a Korean immigrant named Ri Sam Pei in the early seventeenth century,[2] when the manufacture of blue and white in Japan may be presumed to have started. But no pieces of Japanese blue and white have so far been put forward with any documentary claim to belong to the early seventeenth century, to say nothing of the sixteenth.

In the absence of any more definite evidence than this, we are compelled at present to rely on comparisons, on grounds of style and technique, with datable Chinese porcelain, supplemented by informa-

---

[1] *A Guide to the Pottery and Porcelain of the Far East*, British Museum, 1924.

[2] Hobson gives the date as 1605. Koyama in a recent paper, *Sanzai, Outline of Japanese Ceramic Art History*, 1953, gives the date as 1616.

tion provided by inventories and descriptions of Japanese porcelain i n the possession of wealthy Europeans during the seventeenth century. Some reliable evidence of the kind is provided by the collections buil t up at Hampton Court and the Johanneum at Dresden. They contained many pieces acquired during the last quarter of the seventeent h century and we may be fairly sure that some of the Japanese piece s were acquired as early as 1680. These early pieces were dishes, bow ls and vases, often in European shapes, decorated sometimes in under - glaze blue and sometimes in enamels described by the name of th e potter family of Kakiemon,[1] who are said to have introduced thes e beautiful enamelled wares sometime during the second quarter o f the seventeenth century. Sometimes pieces are found with both under - glaze blue and enamel decoration. The underglaze blue is inferior t o the contemporary Chinese blue. Not only is the colour greyish but it tends to run badly, so much so that the later potters used gilt outline s to hide the edges of the blue. This may explain why the Japanes e used overglaze blue, which they could control, more than the Chines e and developed it to a higher state of perfection.

In spite of the lack of positive evidence of manufacture of Japanes e blue and white much before 1680, a comparison of the designs wi th those of the corresponding Chinese pieces gives us strong grounds f or thinking that some of the Japanese pieces were made in the earl y seventeenth century. The dish (I) closely resembles some Chinese export dishes of the late sixteenth century, both in its central subject and in the surrounding panels of flower sprays and tasselled emblems, and may tentatively be accepted as a piece of Arita ware made during the first quarter of the seventeenth century.

In addition to the blue and white made at Arita, some early war es were also made at Kutani. The potteries at Kutani, in the province of Kaga, are said by Koyama[2] to have started between 1640 and 1650, when Goto Saijiro was sent to Arita by one of the princes of Kaga to learn the methods of manufacture. The early Kutani wares, as we understand them, are less refined and more vigorous than the Arita wares, but the borderline between the two is sometimes very narrow and although we can find distinguishing qualities in the enamelled wares, the attribution of the blue and white wares presents great difficulty.

[1] Jenyns, 'The Polychrome Wares associated with the Potters Kakiemon,' *O.C.S. Trans.*, 1937–38. Koyama, *loc. cit.*, states that Sakaida Kakiemon started to make red-enamelled wares in 1643.
[2] *Loc. cit.*

(I) *Plate* 92A.

The second dish illustrated (1) is a typical example of Arita ware made in the second half of the seventeenth century. The well-modelled fluted edge has a brown dressing, a common feature of Chinese dishes made in the mid-seventeenth century. The two bottles and ewer (2) serve to illustrate the differences, as we understand them, between Arita and Kutani. The square bottle and the ewer have border designs which are typical of the Arita wares, both blue and white and polychrome, and their shapes both show European influence. This is not surprising in view of the close trading relationship between the Japanese and the Dutch, whose first settlement, on the island of Deshima, near Nagasaki, took place in 1641. The round bottle, on the other hand, has a purely Japanese shape, and the free design of grasses and arum leaves is in a style that we associate with the Kutani potteries. As a broad generalisation, we may say that the Kutani wares show far less European influence than do the Arita wares. The three small pieces (3) illustrate further the influence of Europe on the shapes of pieces made by the Arita potteries.

The early Japanese blue and white can generally be easily distinguished from the contemporary Chinese. As has already been pointed out, the blue decoration is impure in colour and tends to run badly, in contrast with the Chinese blue which is much better in colour and which, even in the coarser export wares, is generally painted with great clarity. The Japanese porcelain is also coarser in quality and the glaze generally rather greyish with a texture rather uneven, which has sometimes been likened to that of muslin. These descriptions apply to the normal wares. Exceptional pieces (4) particularly those made towards the end of the seventeenth or the beginning of the eighteenth centuries, may be found of fine quality in body and glaze, although rarely with the quality of blue found in a good Chinese piece. It must be remembered, however, that the Japanese potters were in general more interested in the more vigorous and coarser types of Chinese porcelain, such as the non-Imperial T'ien Ch'i wares, and even the provincial wares of Swatow, rather than the less vigorous and more refined types which formed the standard wares exported to Europe during the K'ang Hsi period. Comparison of the Japanese pieces with the provincial wares shows sometimes a remarkable resemblance. The larger Japanese pieces, including most of the dishes, have been fired on spurs, a practice very rarely followed in Chinese blue and white. It has frequently been stated[1] that Japanese porcelain was fired before being glazed and not, like the Chinese,

[1] Hobson, *loc. cit.*, Burton, *Porcelain, Its Art and Manufacture*.

---

(1) *Plate* 92B; (2) *Plates* 93A, 93B and 94A; (3) *Plate* 94B; (4) *Plate* 95A.

(a) *Outside view*

(b) *Inside view*

J. SHONZUI WARE, CH'UNG-CHÊNG PERIOD. DIAM. 7.1 in.

Cover of the jar in Colour Plate H

glazed before being fired. But such evidence as is available does not support this view.[1]

Some Japanese blue and white was exported to Europe during the second half of the seventeenth century and the eighteenth, but the main interest was in the Kakiemon and the so-called 'Old Imari' wares, in which underglaze blue with red and green enamels and copious gilding were used in heavily brocaded designs. The influence of Japanese blue and white on European ceramics was small compared with that of the Chinese.

Blue and white was also made at Okawachi, a few miles from Arita, under the patronage of the Prince of Nabeshima, and is generally known by his name. The potteries are said to have been started round about 1660 with the help of potters from other Hizen kilns, but the earliest pieces known in the West, and those regarded as typical of Nabeshima, seem to have been made in the first half of the eighteenth century. They are generally decorated in underglaze blue and enamels of turquoise green, red and pale yellow. A feature of the dishes is their deep foot rims decorated with a comb pattern in underglaze blue. The designs, as Honey has pointed out,[2] are on conventional lines, 'but on examination reveal a subtle rhythm and richness of invention.' Blue and white Nabeshima is rather scarce, as compared with the coloured wares. A good example is shown in Plate 95B. These attractive wares have been extensively and well copied in modern times.

Another centre of manufacture of blue and white was Mikawachi, also in the province of Hizen. The potteries are said to have been started by Koreans in the seventeenth century but not to have made porcelain until the eighteenth. They were taken under the patronage of Matsura, Prince of Hirado, in 1751. From this date until 1843, according to Hobson, Hirado porcelain was the finest produced in Japan. The porcelain is of fine quality in body and glaze, decorated in delicate style in a pale blue with such subjects as flowers, landscapes and human figures. The potters excelled in moulded, carved and pierced designs, generally applied to small intimate objects such as boxes and incense burners (I).

In the first half of the nineteenth century blue and white eggshell porcelain was made at Seto and other factories. It shows great technical skill but its artistic merits are small. Towards the end of the century the introduction of European production methods caused the dis-

[1] J. M. Plumer, *F.E.C.B.*, March, June, September 1951.
[2] *Ceramic Art of China*, p. 187.

(I) *Plates* 96A, 96B.

appearance of the small family-owned potteries working on traditional lines and replaced them by modern factories which produced meretricious wares in competition with the west. Nevertheless there still remained a number of individual potters who, in the particular field of blue and white, contented themselves with making fine copies of the earlier Chinese wares. Some of these are very good indeed, and are likely to deceive the unwary or even, at times, the expert.

THE DATING AND ATTRIBUTION OF ORIENTAL BLUE AND WHITE

There can be no doubt that oriental porcelain presents special difficulties in identification. There are two main reasons for this. In the first place, the manufacture of the porcelain is spread over a much longer period than, say, that of European porcelain. The period of development of the latter, a mere two hundred years, is less than one-fifth of that of Chinese porcelain. Blue and white itself covers a period of over six hundred years, during which the methods of manufacture, as far as we can tell from examination of pieces and such details as have been handed down to us, changed little. In the second place, the traditional reverence for the past, a vital force in oriental art, resulted in copies of earlier wares being made at almost all periods. Sometimes the copies are easily distinguished from the originals, even by students with little experience. At other times, the copies are so good that the number of attributions is equalled by the number of experts consulted.

The difficulties of identification should not, however, be overstressed. The first stage in the process of identification is to place the piece in a particular known group and this can generally be done with a little experience for most of the pieces that we come across. A very small part, less than 5 per cent of the whole, will be difficult to place. Their identification will call for detailed study and discussion.

Once the piece is identified as belonging to a particular group, the more difficult problem arises of placing it within the group. For example a piece with the Wan Li mark may be identified as belonging to the period. But the Wan Li reign lasted forty-six years and the keen collector will want to say whether it belongs to the earlier or later part of the reign. Comparison with pieces bearing the mark of the previous Emperor Lung Ch'ing, who reigned for only five years (1567–1572), often enables early pieces of Wan Li to be identified.

The earliest pieces of blue and white—those belonging to the fourteenth and fifteenth centuries—are the most difficult to date exactly. We do not yet know how to distinguish pieces made during the different parts of the fourteenth century, and even in the fifteenth century unmarked pieces can often not be dated to within fifty years or more, in our present state of knowledge.

The identification of blue and white pieces calls for examination of the material of the body and glaze, the method of potting and the finish of the piece, the shape, the decoration, including the colour of the blue, and the mark. Each characteristic provides some evidence which contributes to the final assessment of the piece. In the following pages an attempt will be made to describe some of the variations in these characteristics that occur in the different periods. But it must be strongly stressed that the account given here is necessarily incomplete, that verbal descriptions are inadequate and that nothing can replace continuous handling and study of pieces of all periods.

Material of body and glaze

Except for the soft paste porcelain of the eighteenth century, the material from which oriental blue and white porcelain was made is substantially the same for all periods. A description of the method of manufacture is given in Chapter I. The body of the earliest pieces of the fourteenth century, excavated pieces made for Chinese use, appears to be somewhat softer than that of the later pieces. Apart from this, the same hard body seems to have been used generally. The bodies vary a good deal in quality, which depends on the constitution of the raw material and the amount of care taken in its purification. The fourteenth century bodies are rather more greyish than the fifteenth and not quite so fine in texture. From the fifteenth century onwards the material of the finest pieces is pure white, of fine grain and smooth to the touch. During the sixteenth century the quality deteriorated and the deterioration continued in the early part of the seventeenth century. There was an improvement again in the Transition Wares, which was maintained in the early part of the Ch'ing dynasty. In the second half of the eighteenth century there was a deterioration which became very rapid in the nineteenth, when the lowest level in quality was reached. The bodies of Japanese and Korean blue and white are generally coarser and more greyish than those of Chinese pieces.

The part of the body exposed to the kiln often burns a reddish brown, the result of iron impurity in the paste. This is superficial and is removed by slight wear, such as occurs on foot rims. The unglazed bases of fourteenth and fifteenth century dishes are generally reddish unless, as has frequently happened, the bases have been scoured. As a general rule, Ming pieces of blue and white will be found to be reddish on the exposed parts, while pieces of the Ch'ing period are either white or a pale buff.

66

The glaze, being fired in a reducing atmosphere, always has a bluish or greenish tinge, which varies with the amount of iron impurity and the thickness of the glaze. The fourteenth and fifteenth century wares are generally covered with a thick glaze with a slightly pitted surface described by the term 'orange peel', until we reach the period of Ch'êng Hua, when a thinner and more glossy glaze was used. In the Mohammedan wares of the Chêng Tê period an especially thick glaze was used, which assumes a greenish blue tint. Glazes are generally thicker and deeper in colour for Ming than Ch'ing pieces. The glazes of the K'ang Hsi period (after 1683) are thin, the bases of some dishes and vases having almost a dry appearance. The thin glossy glaze gives a brilliant white background against which the blue decoration stands out boldly. In contrast Ming blue and white is softer and less brilliant. In the eighteenth century the Imperial potters were able to imitate with some success the 'orange peel' glaze of the fifteenth century. The Japanese glazes of the seventeenth and eighteenth centuries are generally inferior in purity and less smooth in texture than the Chinese glazes. The surface has been likened by Hobson to that of muslin.

Methods of potting and finish

Generally the earlier pieces can be distinguished from the later by their individual craftsmanship. The earlier bowls and dishes were hand made, in the strict sense, while the later ones were made by means of special forming tools. The bases of the former are concave as seen from above, and one can often see where the potter's thumbs were when the piece was fashioned. The differences have been discussed in detail by Edgar Bluett.[1] The use of the forming tool, which left the bases quite flat, seems to have started towards the end of the Ming dynasty. The shape of the base is one of the best methods of distinguishing early and late bowls and dishes, but it fails when the piece is small. Indeed it is a general rule that the smaller the piece the more difficult is the identification, because the details of construction and decoration are then less easily distinguished. The bases of jars and vases can sometimes give evidence of period in the same way as those of bowls and dishes.

The treatment of the foot rim also shows signs of individual craftsmanship in the earlier but not the later pieces. Even Imperial pieces which are thinly potted and of the finest quality often reveal the individual potter's touch. Non-Imperial pieces naturally show the craftsman's work more clearly, because little attempt has been made to 'clean up' his work. Thus the knife marks in fashioning the foot

[1] *Ming and Ch'ing Porcelains*, 1933.

rim are easily seen and even radial marks on the base caused by the turning tool, although covered by the glaze, are often visible in sixteenth-century non-Imperial wares.

The shape of the foot rim is often a good general guide. The earliest blue and white dishes and bowls had unglazed bases and were fired resting on their bases. There was therefore no need for a deep foot rim and we find that the foot rims are shallow, broad-based and wedge-shaped. In the fifteenth century the practice of glazing the bases was introduced and first the smaller and then the larger pieces were so glazed until by the end of the century only the very large dishes were made with unglazed bases.[1] The foot rims of the early dishes with glazed bases are usually deep and undercut, this feature being particularly marked in the pieces of the second half of the fifteenth century. The early deep foot rims were necessary to give clearance for the curved bases and the introduction of the forming tool to give flat bases enabled the depth of the foot rim to be reduced. Thus we generally find shallower foot rims from the seventeenth century onwards. During the first half of the seventeenth century there was a tendency for the foot rims to be cut square, a feature that may be noticed in the dishes of the T'ien Ch'i period. Japanese dishes and bowls of the seventeenth and eighteenth centuries, except those of small diameter, were fired on spurs and foot rims are found to be shallow. Chinese blue and white was hardly ever fired on spurs and the presence of spur marks thus provides a good indication of provenance.

Vases and jars are generally thrown in a number of pieces, which are luted together before being fired. In Ming pieces the joins can generally be easily discerned, while in Ch'ing pieces close examination is needed to discern them. Methods of manufacture of some types also changed. For example, flasks of the type known as 'full moon' (1) and in the shape of a double gourd (2) when early are moulded in horizontal sections while eighteenth-century copies are moulded vertically. The foot rims of the double gourd vases are formed integrally in the early pieces but are added separately in the later. There is a tendency in the earlier wares to use a larger number of sections than in the later. In some Ming vases of moderate size as many as five sections have been used.[2]

Shape

Shape is not such a reliable criterion in Ming and Ch'ing pieces as in

[1] Bahrami, *O.C.S. Trans.*, 1949–50, refers to a large Chêng Tê dish with unglazed base, and large Chia Ching dishes with such bases are known.
[2] See Jenyns, *Ming Pottery and Porcelain*, Plates 102A, 102B.

(1) *Plate* 30A; (2) *Plate* 31A.

the wares of the Sung, T'ang and earlier dynasties. In the latter deliberate copies of earlier wares were seldom made and the shape provides a valuable guide to the period. On the other hand, most of the shapes used in the early blue and white wares persisted through the Ming and Ch'ing dynasties, and although there were minor changes of shape which tend to indicate the period these are sometimes so small as to be masked by the slight distortions which occur in manufacture and firing. The *mei p'ing*, for example, depends for its effect on subtle changes of outline. Two such vases, one belonging to the fifteenth century and the other to the eighteenth, in Mrs. Clark's collection, are remarkably close in shape.[1] The shape of the latter is not at all typical of the later period and we may conjecture that a particularly careful attempt to copy the earlier piece was made.

In the first half of the seventeenth century a number of new shapes, the result of European influence, were introduced, including cylindrical vases and jugs with shapes based on silver prototypes. The shapes of the early Japanese vases also show European influence.

Decoration

The colour of the blue is the first feature to be considered. While certain colours are typical of particular periods—and the dark purplish blue of the Chia Ching period may be given as an example—there are always considerable variations in each period. We find this variation even in the early wares. The large pieces made in the second half of the fourteenth century vary from a brilliant dark purplish blue through a pure ultramarine to a dull pale greyish blue.

The variation in colour no doubt depended to some extent on the availability of the imported 'Mohammedan blue', but also on the conditions of firing. Bowls of Imperial Hsüan Tê make are known in which the blue of the design on the outside of the bowl is a pure purplish blue, while inside it is a dark greyish blue, almost black in places.

As far as the fourteenth and fifteenth century wares are concerned it is the unevenness of the colour, the presence of black streaks and patches, the 'heaped and piled' effect caused by the sinking in of the pigment where it has been applied thickly, which help most of all to identify them. The presence of black dots on the lower sides of the outlines on many pieces also helps in identification. These qualities, all the result of technical imperfections, gives these early pieces a character that makes them attractive to many collectors. Any fourteenth or early fifteenth-century pieces that do not exhibit some of

[1] See an article by Bluett, 'Chinese Pottery and Porcelain in the Collection of Mr. and Mrs. Alfred Clark,' *Apollo*, March 1934.

these technical imperfections should be regarded with the greatest suspicion. For some reason, not at present understood, better control of the blue was obtained by the second half of the century and by the time of the Ch'êng Hua, and particularly the Hung Chih period, an even blue colour was obtained. The actual colour of the latter period was poor, but by the time of Chêng Tê an even colour of good quality was obtainable.

Attempts to imitate the 'heaped and piled' effect and the dots in the outlines were made in the latter part of the Ming dynasty, but they are not convincing and it was not until the eighteenth century that good imitations began to be made. Even then the copies are rarely good enough to deceive, although some, such as the eighteenth century *mei p'ing* already referred to, are extremely good. It should be mentioned that a few genuine fifteenth-century pieces seem to have had additional dots added to the outline. One such piece has already been referred to (1).

The technical control in the application of the blue pigment reached by the beginning of the sixteenth century enabled the potters from then onwards to obtain a good and even colour, although there were still considerable variations, no doubt the result of the degree of care given to the preparation of the cobalt oxide and the conditions of firing. A dark purplish blue was favoured during the Chia Ching period and many of the Imperial pieces, not only of this period but of the succeeding reigns Lung Ch'ing and Wan Li, are of this colour. But many pieces of Imperial make do not reach the standard laid down, while the non-Imperial wares are generally greyish. Towards the end of the century a pale silvery blue was popular and many of the pieces exported to Europe are decorated in this colour. In the seventeenth century the colour was greyish, except for the Transition Wares, which are decorated in a fine purplish blue somewhat paler than the Chia Ching blue, and a group of pieces made in the middle of the century (up to the early years of K'ang Hsi), which copied very well the Chia Ching colour. Many of these bear the Chia Ching mark and were once thought to belong to the period.[1] But the style of drawing and the calligraphy of the mark proclaim their seventeenth-century origin. Many of them have had a brown dressing applied to the rim, a popular feature of seventeenth-century wares. The presence of such a dressing in a blue and white piece is an almost certain proof that it is not earlier than the seventeenth century.

The typical K'ang Hsi wares, of the middle period, vary a good deal

[1] See p. 42.

(1) *Plate* 22B.

in colour, the best being a pure cobalt blue, less purplish than that popular in the Ming dynasty. The distinguishing feature is the sharpness of the drawing and the clarity of the white background, for which the thinner glaze is mainly responsible. These qualities persisted to some extent in the Yung Chêng period, (except for the deliberate copies of fifteenth-century pieces), but later in the eighteenth century the deterioration in the colour of the blue, as well as in the glaze and paste, became very marked.

The blue of the early Japanese blue and white by comparison with that of the contemporary Chinese porcelain, is poor. Where the pigment is thin the colour is greyish blue, sometimes with a touch of purple and where thick it becomes almost black. The colour also tends to run beyond the outlines.

In considering the artistic qualities of the decoration we must bear in mind that, even from the earliest period of blue and white, fairly large numbers of pieces were made to each design, and no doubt a number of potters and painters were employed on each. We sometimes think that we can trace the hand of the same artist in different pieces, but generally we find considerable differences in treatment and quality of pieces to the same design. For example, the dishes decorated with a bunch of lotus and other water plants tied with a ribbon (1), of which a large number are known, vary enormously in quality. Some are superb, while others give the impression that they were painted by apprentices. We must not therefore, in assessing pieces, be led to assume that because the drawing is inferior the piece is necessarily later. On the other hand, we can often detect a deterioration in style which comes from a lack of the inspiration that governed the original design. The boldly conceived border of serpentine waves found, for example, in the David vases (2), was copied throughout the later periods with steady deterioration. We find it eventually, almost unrecognisable, in the so-called 'ammonite scrolls' of the Isnik dishes of the early seventeenth century. An extreme example is found in the dishes decorated with the 'three friends', in which the rocks of the fifteenth century (3) are converted in the nineteenth century into a kind of Victorian grotto, complete with entrance door.[1]

Reference has already been made to the changes in style of painting that took place in the second half of the fifteenth century. In the earlier wares the outlines were simply used as a general indication of

[1] See *Catalogue of O.C.S. Exhibition of Blue and White Porcelain*, 1953–54, Plate 17 (No. 313).

(1) *Plate* 13; (2) *Plate* 6; (3) *Plates* 32A, 32B.

the pattern and broad washes of pigment were applied, while in the later wares carefully drawn outlines were filled in with a uniform wash. No doubt the method of application of the pigment in the earlier wares was dictated by the difficulty of control, but it resulted in a freedom of drawing showing great artistry. The increase in technical control in the later wares, which enabled the outlines to be drawn and filled in more easily, led to a loss of vigour and strength, and to the decline of blue and white in the later part of the Ming dynasty. The control possible in the Ch'ing dynasty was even more complete and we find, for example, in the Yung Chêng copies of Ch'êng Hua blue and white, a mechanical evenness which contrasts with the variety of tone of the earlier wares.

While generally there is a loss of vigour as we pass from the fourteenth century through the Ming and Ch'ing dynasties, this mainly occurs in the porcelain made in the Imperial potteries. There was a continual renewal of vigour in the non-Imperial porcelain, not only in that made in Kiangsi but also in that made in the provinces, such as Fukien. Thus we find great difficulty at times in distinguishing non-Imperial simple wares, decorated with such subjects as landscapes or flower sprays, of the sixteenth century from similar pieces of the fourteenth and early fifteenth centuries.

Many of the border patterns of the early blue and white were repeated in later wares and a study of the changes in style can help in dating the piece. The wave border has already been mentioned. The petal-shaped borders, generally known as 'false gadroons', changed a great deal, as can be seen even from the small number of examples illustrated in this book, from the simple strong designs of the earlier wares to the mechanical fussy designs of the sixteenth century. Other borders, such as the key fret and the 'Classic scroll', show the same kind of changes. The latter has lost much of its early beauty even by the end of the fifteenth century.

The dragon is one of the commonest subjects of decoration in Chinese porcelain. It appears on the earliest wares and continues throughout the whole period of development, both on Imperial and non-Imperial wares. Although there were variations in the representations of dragons in each period, there was a tendency for the same characteristics to be used in a particular period, especially for Imperial wares. Some account of this subject has been given by Cammann.[1] We may note the fourteenth-century dragons, with their antler-like horns (1) generally without a mane, which is such a

[1] *China's Dragon Robes*, New York, 1952.

(1) *Plates* 3, 6, 7, 24.

K. K'ANG HSI MARK AND PERIOD.   DIAM. 10.5 in.
Mr. R. F. A. Riesco
See page 46

prominent feature of the dragons of the Hsüan Tê and later periods (1), the curiously drawn dragons of the Hung Chih and Chêng Tê periods, with their two eyes side by side in a profile view (2), and the individualistic dragons, with their long feelers and bushy manes, of the later Imperial K'ang Hsi period (3).

Mention has been made in the text of other individual features in blue and white decoration which assist in identification. They include the method of drawing the flower scrolls in the fourteenth century,[1] and the style of drawing the grass and clouds in the Transition Wares.[2]

Japanese and Chinese blue and white can usually be distinguished easily by the quality of the glaze, colour and method of firing, without reference to the style of painting, but there is one group that presents difficulties. The rather crude Chinese wares, mostly dishes, of the second quarter of the seventeenth century, as typified by the pieces with T'ien Ch'i mark, were exported to Japan, where they were held in high admiration. Copies of these wares, and pieces in their style were made in Japan and are difficult to distinguish from the Chinese wares. The rather matt glaze, the dull greyish blue, and the roughness of finish are very similar and the simple designs, drawn with vigour, are similar in feeling. When the Japanese pieces are fired on spurs they can of course be easily identified, but it seems likely that some of the early Japanese dishes were fired in the Chinese fashion and these present a real problem of identification.

A brief reference to the vast field of subjects used by the Chinese potter is all that can be included here. For a full treatment, at any rate as applied to the later Chinese wares, the reader is referred to Honey's *Guide to the Later Chinese Porcelain*. The subjects range from the more formal ones, such as lotus scrolls, dragons and phoenixes, to the informal landscapes such as we find in the sixteenth and seventeenth century non-Imperial wares. The decorative motives have their origin in ceremonial or legend, and a wide knowledge of Chinese history and culture is often necessary to appreciate the significance of some detail of decoration. The influence of the dominant religion at the time may help in the dating of pieces. We have seen, for example, the Mohammedan influence in the designs of Chêng Tê and the Taoist influence in those of Chia Ching, which frequently depict the eight immortals and the emblems of immortality. The use of symbolism became even more extensive in the archaising periods of the eighteenth century, Yung Chêng and Ch'ien Lung.

[1] See pp. 17, 18.
[2] See p. 41.

(1) *Plates* 25, 26B, 29A; (2) *Plates* 39, 46; (3) *Plate* 74.

Marks

The most important marks on Chinese blue and white are the reign marks in the form known as the *nien hao*. In its full form it consists of six characters. The first pair refer to the dynasty, e.g. Ta Ming, the great Ming dynasty, the second pair to the reign, e.g. Hsüan Tê, and the third pair are in the form *nien chih* or *nien tsao*, 'made in the period of.' Sometimes the first pair of characters is omitted and sometimes the second pair. The reign marks that occur on blue and white of the Ming and Ch'ing dynasties are given on pp. 81 and 82 respectively.

The custom of using the *nien hao* on blue and white seems to have been established in the reign of Hsüan Tê. No pieces of blue and white bearing earlier marks than this have, as yet, any solid claim to acceptance, nor do we know of any marked pieces with such a claim made between the reigns of Hsüan Tê and Ch'êng Hua (1435 to 1465). It was not long before the use of former reign marks came into use, not only for pieces imitating earlier wares, but also as a means of adding lustre to the ordinary wares of the period. The confused situation resulting from this practice seems at first sight to be beyond resolution, but a careful study of a large number of pieces that can be identified by other means enables us to get very useful information from the marks and, as a broad generalisation, to use the marks as a means of identification, even when the piece does not belong to the period of the mark.

Generally the calligraphy of the marks of pieces belonging to the same group, such as, for example, the so-called Ch'êng Hua 'palace bowls', or the Mohammedan Chêng Tê wares, are remarkably similar to each other. It is possible, as Brankston has suggested for the former, that a single painter was responsible for all the inscriptions in each group. But it seems more likely that there were a number of painters who were trained together and who would therefore use a similar type of calligraphy.

There are certain features in the characters of the *nien hao* which distinguish the marks of different periods. A good deal of valuable work has been done on marks of the Ming dynasty by Edgar Bluett,[1] from which certain clear distinctions emerge, particularly in the calligraphy of the second character of the *nien hao*, i.e. *Ming*. There are a number of exceptions to the rules which he lays down but the rules apply to by far the greater part of the marks available for examination. Another character which shows great variation is the last in the *nien hao*, i.e. *chih*. This will be discussed later when the marks of particular periods are examined.

The characters of the *nien hao* are usually arranged in two columns

[1] *O.C.S. Trans.*, 1935–36, and 1942–43.

of three characters each, read, of course, from right to left, but they are sometimes arranged in a single line and sometimes in a circle. From the K'ang Hsi period onwards the characters are often found in three columns of two characters each. Sometimes the marks, particularly in the Ch'ing dynasty from the reign of Yung Chêng onwards, are written in an archaic script known as seal character. Seal characters rarely occur on blue and white in the Ming dynasty, except in marks of the Yung Lo period, found on a group of bowls made in the first half of the seventeenth century.[1]

A number of photographs of marks taken from pieces whose dates are well established are reproduced in Plates 97 to 100. The series of marks of the earlier Ming reigns on original pieces and later copies should be studied. It is not possible to go fully into all the points of detail and indeed many more photographs would be needed for this. But the following points may be noted. The variations in the Ming character are generally consistent with those noted by Bluett,[2] but the marks of the Ch'êng Hua period provide many exceptions. Indeed the calligraphy of this reign is generally poor by fifteenth-century standards, being far inferior to that of Hsüan Tê or of the later reigns Hung Chih and Chêng Tê. The writing appears to have been done with a wet brush and this itself leads to a lack of clarity. The character *chih* is generally carelessly painted (1). However, the two strokes sloping from right to left at the bottom of the character are distinct, whereas in the K'ang Hsi and Yung Chêng copies they are often made into a single line (2). This character is clearly written in fine calligraphy in the Hung Chih and Mohammedan Chêng Tê pieces (3) and this style of writing was continued into the beginning of the Chia Ching period (4).

The Hsüan Tê marks on pieces of the period are generally of high quality (5). The mark on a small dish of Imperial quality made round about 1500 (6), although of equally high quality, shows the changes of style that had taken place by the end of the fifteenth century. The mark on a piece belonging to the second half of the sixteenth century (7) is rather slovenly, although not without vigour. The mark on a K'ang Hsi piece, typical of the period (8), is a mere travesty of the original.

A feature of the marks of the Chêng Tê period is the frequent use of the four-character mark *Chêng Tê nien chih*, which is hardly ever found in Imperial blue and white of other periods, although there are

[1] See p. 21.
[2] *Loc. cit.*

(1) *Cf. Plates* 98A, B, C with *Plates* 97A, G; (2) *Plate* 98E, 99C; (3) *Plates* 97G, 98G; (4) *Plate* 99A; (5) *Plates* 97A, B, C; (6) *Plate* 97D; (7) *Plate* 97E; (8) *Plate* 97F.

75

a few exceptions. Another is a variation in the writing of the *nien* character, in which the small vertical stroke is omitted and an additional small horizontal stroke added (1). This particular mark is that of the Imperial dish of Plate 46A. This variant is a common feature in non-Imperial marks from the beginning of the sixteenth century onwards (2) but its frequent appearance on some Imperial Chêng Tê pieces and its absence from others is very puzzling. It is found occasionally on pieces with the Hsüan Tê mark, but these belong to the early part of the sixteenth century. The use of the character *tsao* (3) occurs throughout the Ming dynasty, generally, but not always on non-Imperial wares.

The later Ming marks do not present so many problems, but we are becoming aware of many seventeenth-century copies of pieces of the Chia Ching period, and a study of the marks on originals and copies can help in identification (4). The calligraphy of some of the seventeenth-century copies resembles that of the early K'ang Hsi period.

The calligraphy of the K'ang Hsi period itself has a number of distinct phases. The earliest pieces are marked in a bold heavy style well represented by Plate 99F (although this is not a *nien hao*) and Plate 99G. The marks of the middle period are rather loose and slovenly (5) while those of the last period are neat and precise (6). The latest type of mark is most often found in peach bloom pieces and those decorated in designs in copper red. It is not common on blue and white.

The marks of the later reigns of the Ch'ing dynasty do not call for any special comments. The marks of Yung Chêng and Ch'ien Lung, both in ordinary script and seal characters, have been copied in recent times with great fidelity. The copies are rarely of blue and white, the more popular Imperial self-colours and *famille rose* being chosen for imitation.

A number of pieces of blue and white have marks or inscriptions which give the actual year of manufacture. These marks are of two kinds. In the first, the year of a particular reign is given, e.g., the fifteenth year of Wan Li. This type of mark generally occurs on pieces made for presentation to a temple, and the inscription often includes the day and month, as well as the year, on which the piece was painted. The inscriptions on the David vases, (7) the Hung Chih vase (8) and the Wan Li stove jar (9) are of this kind. The second kind of mark gives what is known as a cyclical date. The system of dating is fully described in Hobson's *Wares of the Ming Dynasty*. Briefly, the Chinese cycle consists of sixty years which, for the period with which we are concerned, started in 1324, 1384, 1444 and so on. Each year in

---

(1) *Plate* 98I; (2) *Plate* 97I; (3) *Plate* 97I; (4) *Plates* 99A, B, C; (5) *Plate* 99H; (6) *Plate* 99I; (7) *Plate* 6; (8) *Plate* 38; (9) *Plate* 54.

the cycle is defined by two characters. Sometimes the cyclical year mark is associated with a reign, as in the example already noted (1) and the Chia Ching wine jar (2) which is dated 1561. But sometimes the reign mark is not given and the actual year of manufacture may be uncertain by sixty years or some multiple of sixty. The Transition vase (3) has such a cyclical mark. We can say that the date of manufacture, however, was almost certainly 1636. The only possible alternative would be 1696 and the shape, method of manufacture and, above all, the style of drawing, rule out the later date.

Many other types of marks than date marks were used on Chinese blue and white. These include hall marks, potter's marks and marks of good wish, dedication and commendation. For further information on these Honey's *Ceramic Art of China* and other standard works should be consulted. From the sixteenth century onwards symbols and emblems were sometimes used in place of the written marks. These became common during the K'ang Hsi period, more so than any other kind of mark. The mark of the hare and the crescent moon (4) is to be found on pieces dating from the middle of the sixteenth century and the so-called 'shop mark' (5), a debased seal mark, is often found on mid-seventeenth-century wares. Of the many other subjects found on K'ang Hsi pieces we may mention an incense burner (*ting*), sacred fungus (*ling chih*), a palm leaf (*chiao yeh*) and a spray of plum blossom.

The marks of Japanese blue and white are of little use as a means of dating the pieces. Chinese reign marks are sometimes used, particularly those of Hsüan Tê, Ch'êng Hua (6) and Wan Li (7). Some of the Chinese hall marks and marks of commendation are also used. The only Japanese mark that appears at all frequently on early blue and white is that of *fuku* (happiness) (8). The marks on Japanese porcelain are often enclosed in a single rather than a double ring (9). The use of a single ring in Chinese porcelain is very rare.

General

The practice of burying pottery and porcelain in tombs had almost died out by the time of the Yüan dynasty, but some of the earliest blue and white pieces are excavated wares. As a result of burial, the surface of an excavated piece is generally slightly eroded, and because in many instances the piece has lain on one side, the erosion will be found to be worse on one side than the other. A number of blue and white fakes purporting to belong to the Sung period have been made, in which the effect of burial has been simulated by acid

(1) *Plate* 99F; (2) *Plate* 51; (3) *Plate* 60B; (4) *Plate* 100E; (5) *Plate* 100F; (6) *Plate* 100G; (7) *Plate* 99E; (8) *Plate* 100H; (9) *Plate* 100G.

treatment. This has given a more marked and even degradation of the surface than occurs in real burial. A comparison of one of these fakes with a piece that has been buried for hundreds of years shows how unsuccessful the forger has been.

Old pieces that have not been buried—and these comprise nearly all the blue and white that we have been discussing—will show signs of wear. The practice of preserving precious pieces of porcelain in boxes and only handling them on special occasions was prevalent in China, and these pieces will show much less wear than pieces that have been in common use. But they should certainly show some wear. Pieces showing little or no wear should in the first place be regarded with suspicion, and their other characteristics should be examined with particular care. Wear can be simulated and there are many examples of artificially worn pieces of blue and white. Such pieces are often found with long even scratches applied in the same direction instead of scratches of different intensities and in different directions. A genuinely worn piece will show the greatest amount of wear on projecting parts, edges or in places where it is naturally handled. A study of the wear in relation to the shape and use of the piece will generally indicate whether the wear is real or simulated.

An attempt has been made to describe some of the qualities that distinguish oriental blue and white belonging to the different periods. This would not be easy, even if deliberate attempts to copy earlier pieces had not been the practice both in China and Japan. As it is, the student not only has to be familiar with the normal characteristics of each period, but also to detect copies in which the maker has deliberately attempted to simulate the earlier characteristics. In the battle of wits between himself and the copyist, the student can be certain that there is some weakness in the copyist's armour, if only he can find it. It may be in the type of glaze, the method of construction or the method of application of the pigment. Perhaps the most difficult things to copy are the technical defects which result from the potter's lack of complete control of his medium, and these should be closely watched.

The vast range covered by oriental blue and white in which, as we have seen, copies good and bad of earlier wares were made at all periods, makes the task of the collector a difficult one. To understand fully any particular group of blue and white it is necessary to know a good deal about the rest. In particular, the early Chinese blue and white of the fourteenth and fifteenth centuries cannot be properly understood without knowledge of the later copies of the Ming and Ch'ing dynasties. The collector may, in despair, decide to collect just those pieces that he admires and not be too particular about their provenance. He will get much enjoyment from this. But a deeper appreciation will come from a knowledge of the subtle points that distinguish oriental blue and white of different periods, potteries and countries.

APPENDIX
REIGN MARKS OF MING AND CH'ING DYNASTIES

MING DYNASTY

年製洪武
HUNG WU
(1368–98)

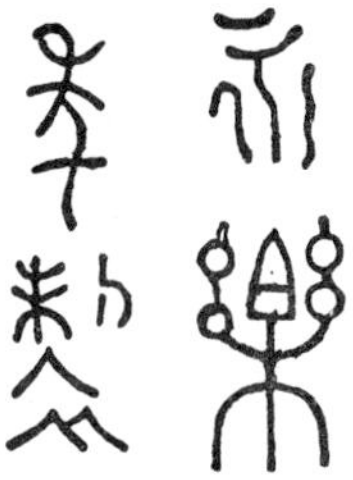

YUNG LO
(1403–24)

年製永樂
YUNG LO
(1403–24)

德年製大明宣
HSÜAN TÊ
(1426–35)

化年製大明成
CH'ÊNG HUA
(1465–87)

治年製大明弘
HUNG CHIH
(1488–1505)

德年製大明正
ĆHÊNG TÊ
(1506–21)

靖年製大明嘉
CHIA CHING
(1522–66)

慶年製大明隆
LUNG CH'ING
(1567–72)

曆年製大明萬
WAN LI
(1573–1619)

啟年製大明天
T'IEN CH'I
(1621–27)

年製崇禎
CH'UNG CHÊNG
(1628–43)

CH'ING DYNASTY

治年製 大清順 [seal mark]   熙年製 大清康 [seal mark]

Shun Chih, 1644–1661   K'ang Hsi, 1662–1722

正年製 大清雍 [seal mark]   隆年製 大清乾 [seal mark]

Yung Chêng, 1723–1735   Ch'ien Lung, 1736–1795

年製 嘉慶   光年製 大清道 [seal mark]

Chia Ch'ing, 1796–1820   Tao Kuang, 1821–1850

豐年製 大清咸 [seal mark]   治年製 大清同

Hsien Fêng, 1851–1861   T'ung Chih, 1862–1874

緒年製 大清光 [seal mark]   統年製 大清宣   年製 洪憲

Kuang Hsü, 1875–1908   Hsüan T'ung,   Hung Hsien (1916)
                            1909–1912   (Yüan Shih-kai)

BIBLIOGRAPHY

E. E. BLUETT, *Ming and Ch'ing Porcelains*. London, 1933.

C. R. BOXER, *Fidalgos in the Far East*. The Hague, 1948.

A. BRANKSTON, *Early Ming Wares of Chingtechen*. Peking, 1938.

S. W. BUSHELL, *Oriental Ceramic Art*. New York, 1899. *Description of Chinese Pottery and Porcelain, being a translation of the T'ao Shuo*. Oxford, 1910.

S. CAMMANN, *China's Dragon Robes*. New York, 1952.

T'IEN-TSE CHANG, *Sino-Portuguese Trade from 1514 to 1644*. Leyden, 1944.

R. L. HOBSON, *Wares of the Ming Dynasty*. London, 1925. *Handbook of the Pottery and Porcelain of the Far East, British Museum*. London, 1937 and 1948. *Catalogue of Chinese Pottery and Porcelain in the Collection of Sir Percival David*. London, 1934.

W. B. HONEY, *The Ceramic Art of China and other Countries of the Far East*, London, 1945. *Guide to the Later Chinese Porcelain. in the Victoria and Albert Museum*. London, 1927.

S. JENYNS, *Ming Pottery and Porcelain*. London, 1953. *Later Chinese Porcelain*. London, 1951.

NIHON TŌZI KYŌKAI (edited by), *Ming Blue and White and Enamelled Porcelain*. Tokyo, 1952.

TAKUSHIN KUSHI, *Early Ming Chinese Porcelain*. Tokyo, 1943.

A. LANE, *Islamic Pottery*. London, 1947.

NANNE OTTEMA, *Chineesche ceramiek, handboek geschreven naar aanleitung van de verzamelingen in het Museum het Princessehof te Leewarden*. Amsterdam 1946.

J. A. POPE, *Fourteenth-Century Blue and White in the Topkapu Sarayi Musesi, Istanbul*. Washington, 1952.

E. ROSENTHAL, *Pottery and Ceramics*. London, 1949.

G. R. SAYER, *Ching-tê Chên T'ao Lu, or the Potteries of China, being a translation*. London, 1949.

E. ZIMMERMANN, *Altchinesische Porzellane im Alten Serai*. Berlin, 1930.

The Chinese Exhibition (a commemorative catalogue of the International Exhibition of Chinese Art, 1935–36). London, 1936.

BIBLIOGRAPHY

Illustrated Catalogue of Chinese Government Exhibits for the International Exhibition of Chinese Art in London. Volume II (with a preface by Kuo Pao-Ch'ang). Nanking, 1936.

Catalogue of Exhibition of Ming Blue and White Porcelain held by the Oriental Ceramic Society, 1946. London, 1946.

Ming Blue and White. Philadelphia Museum Bulletin No. 223 (with a preface by Jean Gordon Lee). Philadelphia, 1949.

Detroit Exhibition, Arts of the Ming Dynasty. 1952.

Catalogue of Exhibition of Chinese Blue and White Porcelain held by the Oriental Ceramic Society, 1953–54. London, 1953.

Transactions of the Oriental Ceramic Society, London. From 1921.

Far Eastern Ceramic Bulletin. From 1948.

The Burlington Magazine. From 1902.

Oriental Art. 1948–52.

Additional bibliography for the third edition

JOHN AYERS, 'Some characteristic wares of the Yüan dynasty', *Transactions of the Oriental Ceramic Society,* Vol. 29, 1954–55.

SIR HARRY GARNER, 'Blue and white of the middle Ming period', *Transactions of the Oriental Ceramic Society,* Vol. 27, 1951–53.

G. ST. G. M. GOMPERTZ, *Korean Pottery and Porcelain of the Yi Period.* London, 1968.

SOAME JENYNS, 'The Chinese *ko-sometsuke* and Shonzui wares', *Transactions of the Oriental Ceramic Society,* Vol. 34, 1962–63.

SOAME JENYNS, *Japanese Porcelain.* London, 1965.

LEANDRO and CECILIA LOCSIN, *Oriental Ceramics discovered in the Philippines.* Rutland, Vermont, 1967.

MARGARET MEDLEY, 'Regrouping fifteenth century blue and white', *Transactions of the Oriental Ceramic Society,* Vol. 34, 1962–63.

JOHN ALEXANDER POPE, *Chinese Porcelains from the Ardebil Shrine.* Washington, D.C., 1956.

ORIENTAL CERAMIC SOCIETY, *Catalogue of the Arts of the Ming Dynasty.* London, 1957.

ORIENTAL CERAMIC SOCIETY, *Catalogue of the Arts of the Ch'ing Dynasty.* London, 1964.

INDEX

85

INDEX

1. FIRST HALF OF THE FOURTEENTH CENTURY
A. HT. 3·0 in. *British Museum*
B. HT. 4·6 in.
C. HT. 5·6 in.
See pages 10, 17

2. FIRST HALF OF THE FOURTEENTH CENTURY
A. HT. 4·0 in. *Mr R. H. R. Palmer*
B. HT. 3·0 in. *Mr R. F. A. Riesco*
C. DIAM. 6·2 in. *Mrs Alfred Clark*
See pages 10, 11

3. FIRST HALF OF THE FOURTEENTH CENTURY
HT. 9·8 in. *Mrs Alfred Clark*
See pages 11, 72

4. FIRST HALF OF THE FOURTEENTH CENTURY
HT. 12·0 in. *British Museum*
See page 11

5. FIRST HALF OF THE FOURTEENTH CENTURY
HT. 9·8 in. *Mrs Alfred Clark*
See pages 11, 17

6. MID-FOURTEENTH CENTURY, DATED 1351
HT. 25·0 in. *David Foundation*
See pages 11, 71, 72, 76

7. MID-FOURTEENTH CENTURY. HT. 17·7 in.
Topkapu Sarayi Müzesi, Istanbul
See pages 17, 72

8. SECOND HALF OF THE FOURTEENTH CENTURY
A. DIAM. 13·4 in. *Topkapu Sarayi Müzesi, Istanbul*
B. DIAM. 18·0 in. *Museum of Eastern Art, Oxford*
See page 17

9. SECOND HALF OF THE FOURTEENTH CENTURY
Museum of Eastern Art, Oxford
A. EXTERIOR VIEW. HT. 6·2 in.
B. INTERIOR VIEW. DIAM. 8·0 in.
See page 17

10. SECOND HALF OF THE FOURTEENTH CENTURY
DIAM. 18·5 in. *Mrs Walter Sedgwick*
See page 17

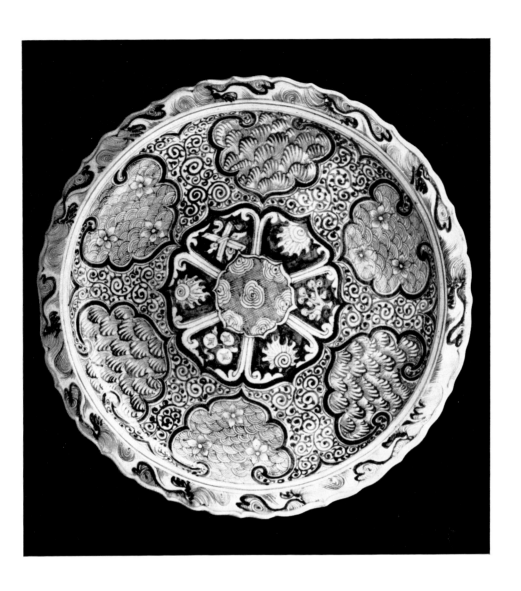

11. SECOND HALF OF THE FOURTEENTH CENTURY
DIAM. 18·1 in. *Topkapu Sarayi Müzesi, Istanbul*
See pages 17, 18

12. SECOND HALF OF THE FOURTEENTH CENTURY
DIAM. 18·0 in. *Victoria and Albert Museum*
See pages 17, 18

13. EARLY FIFTEENTH CENTURY. DIAM. 13·6 in.
Mr Herschel V. Johnson
See pages 18, 71

14. EARLY FIFTEENTH CENTURY. DIAM. 16·7 in.
Cleveland Museum of Art
See page 18

15. EARLY FIFTEENTH CENTURY. DIAM. 14·5 in.
British Museum
See page 18

16. HSÜAN TÊ MARK AND PERIOD. DIAM. 11·0 in.
Victoria and Albert Museum
See pages 13, 17, 22

17. SECOND HALF OF THE FOURTEENTH CENTURY
HT. 15·5 in. *Mrs Alfred Clark*
See page 19

18. SECOND HALF OF THE FOURTEENTH CENTURY
HT. 17·5 in. *Mr Frederick M. Mayer*
See page 19

19. SECOND HALF OF THE FOURTEENTH CENTURY
HT. 15·0 in. *Museum of Fine Arts, Boston*
See page 19

20. SECOND HALF OF THE FOURTEENTH CENTURY
HT. 14·6 in. *Mr Richard B. Hobart*
See page 19

21. SECOND HALF OF THE FOURTEENTH CENTURY
HT. 15·0 in. *Museum of Eastern Art, Oxford*
See page 19

22A. SECOND HALF OF THE FOURTEENTH CENTURY
HT. 11·9 in. *Fitzwilliam Museum, Cambridge*
See page 19
22B. EARLY FIFTEENTH CENTURY. DIAM. 13·9 in.
National Gallery of Victoria, Melbourne
See pages 20, 70

23. EARLY FIFTEENTH CENTURY. HT. 13·5 in.
Royal Ontario Museum of Archaeology, Toronto
See page 19

24. SECOND HALF OF THE FOURTEENTH CENTURY
HT. 14·5 in. *Victoria and Albert Museum*
See pages 19, 72

25. HSÜAN TÊ MARK AND PERIOD. HT. 19·0 in.
Metropolitan Museum of Art
See pages 22, 73

26A. HSÜAN TÊ MARK AND PERIOD. DIAM. 11·0 in.
Mr R. H. R. Palmer
See page 22
26B. EARLY FIFTEENTH CENTURY. HT. 17·5 in.
Mrs Alfred Clark
See pages 22, 73

27. HSÜAN TÊ MARK AND PERIOD
A. HT. 3·5 in. *David Foundation*
B. HT. 3·5 in. *David Foundation*
C. DIAM. 8·8 in.
See page 22

28A. HSÜAN TÊ PERIOD. DIAM. 8·0 in.
Mr Frederick M. Mayer
See page 22
28B. HSÜAN TÊ MARK AND PERIOD. DIAM. 7·2 in.
See page 22

29A. HSÜAN TÊ MARK AND PERIOD. DIAM. 8·1 in.
British Museum
See pages 22, 27, 73
29B. HUNG CHIH MARK AND PERIOD. DIAM. 8·2 in.
David Foundation
See pages 22, 27

30A. EARLY FIFTEENTH CENTURY. HT. 9·7 in.
Mrs Alfred Clark
See pages 22, 68

30B. EARLY FIFTEENTH CENTURY. HT. 5·4 in.
Mrs Alfred Clark
See page 23

30C. HSÜAN TÊ MARK AND PERIOD. DIAM. 6·2 in.
Mr R. F. A. Riesco
See page 23

31. HSÜAN TÊ MARK AND PERIOD
A. HT. 10·0 in. *Mr R. F. A. Riesco*
B. HT. 5·6 in. *Mr R. H. R. Palmer*
See pages 23, 68

32A. HSÜAN TÊ MARK AND PERIOD. DIAM. 7·0 in.
Mrs Alfred Clark
32B. CH'ÊNG HUA MARK AND PERIOD. DIAM. 7·9 in.
Mrs Walter Sedgwick
See pages 25, 52, 71

33. CH'ÊNG HUA MARK AND PERIOD
A. DIAM. 8·5 in. *David Foundation*
B. DIAM. 7·5 in. *David Foundation*
See pages 25, 27

34. CH'ÊNG HUA MARK AND PERIOD. DIAM. 7·2 in.
See page 25

55. CH'ÊNG HUA MARK AND PERIOD
A. DIAM. 5·7 in. *Mr Herschel V. Johnson*
B. DIAM. 5·7 in. *Mr Eugene Bernat*
See page 26

56. LEFT, YUNG CHÊNG MARK AND PERIOD. DIAM. 5·9 in.
RIGHT, CH'ÊNG HUA MARK AND PERIOD. DIAM. 6·0 in.

Mrs Alfred Clark

57. LEFT, CH'ÊNG HUA MARK AND PERIOD. HT. 5·1 in.
RIGHT, YUNG CHÊNG MARK AND PERIOD. HT. 5·1 in.

Sir Percival and Lady David

See pages 26, 49

38. HUNG CHIH PERIOD, DATED 1496. HT. 24·5 in.
David Foundation
See pages 26, 76

39. HUNG CHIH MARK AND PERIOD
A. DIAM. 8·5 in. *Mrs Walter Sedgwick*
B. DIAM. 8·2 in. *Mrs Alfred Clark*
C. DIAM. 8·6 in.
D. BACK OF 39C.
See pages 27, 73

40. SECOND HALF OF THE FIFTEENTH CENTURY
A. DIAM. 6·7 in.
B. DIAM. 11·0 in. *Mr Frederick M. Mayer*
See page 27

41. SECOND HALF OF THE FIFTEENTH CENTURY
A. HT. 4·2 in.
B. HT. 3·7 in. *Mr F. Brodie Lodge*
See page 27

42A. HSÜAN TÊ MARK AND PERIOD. DIAM. 10·1 in.
Mr Richard B. Hobart
42B. CH'ÊNG HUA MARK AND PERIOD. DIAM. 10·2 in.
British Museum
42C. HUNG CHIH MARK AND PERIOD. DIAM. 10·4 in.
42D. CHÊNG TÊ MARK AND PERIOD. DIAM. 7·8 in.
Mrs Otto Harriman
See page 27

45. CHÊNG TÊ MARK AND PERIOD
A. L. 10·2 in. *Royal Ontario Museum, Toronto*
B. HT. 5·9 in. *Mr R. H. R. Palmer*
C. HT. 5·9 in. *Philadelphia Museum of Art*
See pages 28, 29

44. CHÊNG TÊ MARK AND PERIOD
A. L. 9·0 in. *David Foundation*
B. HT. 8·9 in. *British Museum*
See page 29

45. CHÊNG TÊ MARK AND PERIOD. HT. 17·7 in.
David Foundation
See page 29

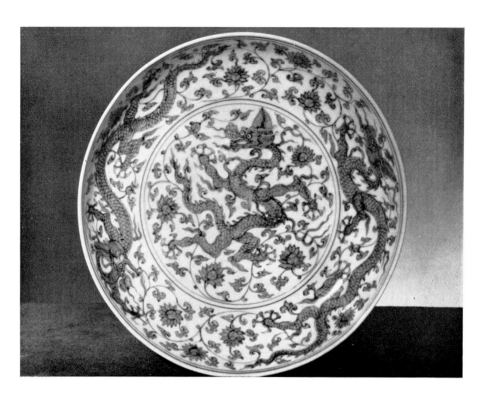

46. CHÊNG TÊ MARK AND PERIOD
A. DIAM. 9·2 in. *Mr R. F. A. Riesco*
B. HT. 4·9 in. *Mr R. H. R. Palmer*
See pages 30, 73

47. CHÊNG TÊ MARK AND PERIOD. HT. 17·8 in.
David Foundation
See page 30

48. CHÊNG TÊ MARK AND PERIOD
A. HT. 7·0 in.
B. HT. 5·5 in.
C. HT. 4·0 in.
Mr Morris S. Whitehouse
See pages 31, 33

49. CHIA CHING MARK AND PERIOD. HT. 17·5 in.
British Museum
See page 32

50. CHIA CHING MARK AND PERIOD
A. HT. 8·2 in.
B. DIAM. 12·2 in.
See pages 32, 33

51. CHIA CHING MARK AND PERIOD, DATED 1561. HT. 12·2 in.
Mr R. F. A. Riesco
See pages 33, 77

52. LUNG CH'ING MARK AND PERIOD
A. DIAM. 5·0 in. *Mr Morris S. Whitehouse*
B. DIAM. 9·1 in. *Mr R. E. Luff*
See page 35

53. WAN LI MARK AND PERIOD
A. DIAM. 5·2 in.
B. DIAM. 11·2 in. *Mr R. H. R. Palmer*
See page 35

54. WAN LI PERIOD, DATED 1618. HT. 14·5 in.
See pages 8, 35, 76

55. WAN LI PERIOD
A. LEFT, WAN LI MARK. DIAM. 5·3 in.
RIGHT, NO MARK. HT. 2·8 in.
B. DATED 1612. DIAM. 3·6 in.
Mr R. F. A. Riesco
C. NO MARK. DIAM. 4·7 in.
Mr H. Knowler
See page 36

56A. CHIA CHING PERIOD, DATED 1557. HT. 9·5 in.
Victoria and Albert Museum
See page 34
56B. SECOND HALF OF THE SIXTEENTH CENTURY
DIAM. 7·9 in.
See page 37

57. SECOND HALF OF THE SIXTEENTH CENTURY
DIAM. 10·7 in.
See pages 35, 36

58. SECOND HALF OF THE SIXTEENTH CENTURY
A. DIAMS. (L. TO R.) 8·0 in., 5·5 in., 8·0 in.
Victoria and Albert Museum
B. HT. 6·4 in., DIAM. 5·5 in. *Mr R. F. A. Riesco*
See page 37

59A. T'IEN CH'I PERIOD, DATED 1621. DIAM. 5·2 in.
Mr R. F. A. Riesco
See page 39
59B. CH'UNG CHENG PERIOD, DATED 1628. DIAM. 7·2 in.
Mr Morris S. Whitehouse

60. TRANSITION PERIOD

A. HT. 7·2 in.

B. DATED 1656. HT. 6·5 in.

Mr Gerald Reitlinger

C. HT. 5·2 in.

61. TRANSITION PERIOD
A. HT. 6·2 in.
B. HT. 5·7 in. *Mr Gerald Reitlinger*
See page 40

62. TRANSITION PERIOD. HT. 18·7 in.
Victoria and Albert Museum
See page 41

63. TRANSITION PERIOD
A. HT. 13·2 in.
B. DIAM. 14·5 in. *Victoria and Albert Museum*
See pages 40, 41

64. TRANSITION PERIOD
A. DATED 1645. DIAM. 5·7 in. *David Foundation*
B. DATED 1655. HT. 8·0 in. *David Foundation*
See pages 41, 44

65. TRANSITION PERIOD
A. DIAMS. (L. TO R.) 3·4 in., 4·0 in., 5·6 in.
Victoria and Albert Museum
B. DIAMS. (L. TO R.) 7·0 in., 4·1 in., 7·0 in
See pages 41, 42

66. K'ANG HSI MARK AND PERIOD
A. DIAM. 6·5 in. *Victoria and Albert Museum*
B. DIAM. 6·5 in. *Victoria and Albert Museum*
See page 45

67. EARLY K'ANG HSI. DIAM. 15·0 in.
Victoria and Albert Museum
See page 45

68. K'ANG HSI PERIOD. CH'ÊNG HUA MARK
DIAM. 8·0 in.
See page 46

69. K'ANG HSI PERIOD
A. HT. 6·7 in. *Mr R. F. A. Riesco*
B. HT. 8·2 in. *Mr J. F. Woodthorpe*
C. DIAM. 8·2 in. *Mr R. F. A. Riesco*
See page 46

70. K'ANG HSI PERIOD. HT. 17·7 in.
Victoria and Albert Museum
See page 46

71. K'ANG HSI PERIOD. HT. 17·0 in.
Victoria and Albert Museum
See page 46

72. K'ANG HSI PERIOD, CH'ÊNG HUA MARK
DIAMS. 10·2 in. *Mr J. F. Woodthorpe*
See page 46

75. K'ANG HSI PERIOD. DIAMS. 6·2 in.

See page 47

74. K'ANG HSI MARK AND PERIOD. HTS. (L. TO R.) 8·2 in.,
2·7 in.
See pages 47, 73

75. YUNG CHÊNG MARK AND PERIOD. HT. 5·0 in.
Mr R. F. A. Riesco
See page 49

76. YUNG CHÊNG MARK AND PERIOD. HT. 20·4 in.
Victoria and Albert Museum
See page 49

77. CH'IEN LUNG MARK AND PERIOD. HT. 13·5 in.
Victoria and Albert Museum
See page 49

78. YUNG CHÊNG MARK AND PERIOD
A. DIAM. 7·2 in.
B. DIAM. 10·5 in.
See page 50

79. CH‘IEN LUNG MARK AND PERIOD
A. HT. 4·6 in.
B. DATED 1786. DIAM. 6·4 in. *Mr B. C. Tattenhall*
See page 50

80. SECOND HALF OF THE EIGHTEENTH CENTURY
A. DIAM. 12·2 in. *Victoria and Albert Museum*
B. DIAM. 18·0 in. *Victoria and Albert Museum*
See page 50

81. SOFT PASTE, EIGHTEENTH CENTURY
A. DIAMS. (L. TO R.) 3·0 in., 3·6 in., 3·3 in. *Mrs Alfred Clark*
B. (L. TO R.) HT. 5·4 in., DIAMS. 4·5 in., 4·4 in.
See page 51

82A. CHIA CH'ING MARK AND PERIOD. DATED 1798
DIAM. 5·7 in. *British Museum*
See pages 50, 52
82B. TAO KUANG MARK AND PERIOD. DIAM. 7·0 in.
British Museum
See page 52

83A. T'UNG CHIH MARK AND PERIOD. DIAM. 9·1 in.
Mr B. C. Tattenhall
83B. KUANG HSÜ MARK AND PERIOD. DIAM. 6·2 in.
See page 52

84A. ANNAMESE, DATED 1450. HT. 21·1 in.
Topkapu Sarayi Müzesi, Istanbul
See pages 8, 54
84B. ANNAMESE. DIAM. 13·0 in.
Mrs Walter Sedgwick
See page 54

85. ANNAMESE. HT. 17·1 in.
Sir David Home
See page 54

86A. ANNAMESE. DIAM. 14·5 in.
Mr Richard de la Mare
86B. 'SWATOW WARE'. DIAM. 13·1 in.
Mr Richard de la Mare
See page 55

87. 'SWATOW WARE'. HT. 14·0 in.
See page 55

88A. 'SWATOW WARE'. DIAM. 15·8 in.
Victoria and Albert Museum
88B. 'SWATOW WARE'. DIAM. 17·6 in.
Mr Soame Jenyns
See page 55

89A. TÊ-HUA WARE. DIAM. 10·2 in.
89B. TÊ-HUA WARE. DIAM. 9·7 in.
Mr Richard de la Mare
See page 56

90. KOREAN. HT. 16·3 in.
Mr Richard de la Mare
See page 58

91A. KOREAN. HT. 7·0 in. *British Museum*
91B. KOREAN. DIAM 9·3 in. *Mr Richard de la Mare*
See page 58

92A. ARITA. DIAM. 8·1 in.
92B. ARITA. DIAM. 10·7 in.
Mr Soame Jenyns
See pages 61, 62

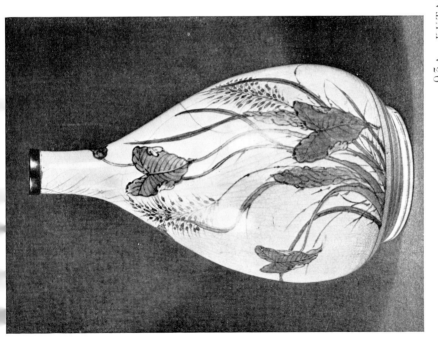

95A. KUTANI. HT. 15·2 in.
Mr Soame Jenyns
95B. ARITA. HT. 10·2 in.
See page 62

94A. ARITA. HT. 11·9 in. *Mr Richard de la Mare*
94B. ARITA. HTS. (L. TO R.) 4·2 in., 3·0 in., 4·5 in.
Mr Soame Jenyns
See page 62

95A. ARITA. DIAM. 10·7 in. *Mr Richard de la Mare*
95B. NABESHIMA. DIAM. 8·0 in. *Mr Richard de la Mare*
See page 62

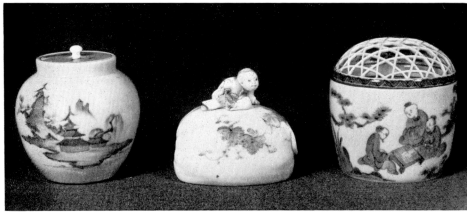

96A. HIRADO. HT. 11·0 in. *Mr Richard de la Mare*
96B. HIRADO. HTS. (L. TO R.) 3·0 in., 2·5 in., 3·2 in.
Mr Soame Jenyns
See page 63

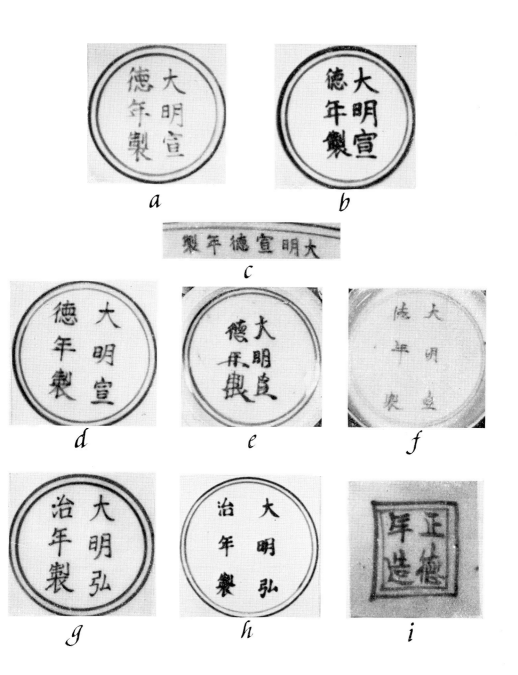

97a, b, c. HSÜAN TÊ MARK AND PERIOD
D. HSÜAN TÊ MARK, *circa* 1500
E. HSÜAN TÊ MARK, SECOND HALF SIXTEENTH CENTURY
F. HSÜAN TÊ MARK, K'ANG HSI PERIOD
G, H. HUNG CHIH MARK AND PERIOD
I. CHÊNG TÊ MARK AND PERIOD. NON-IMPERIAL WARE
See pages 75, 76

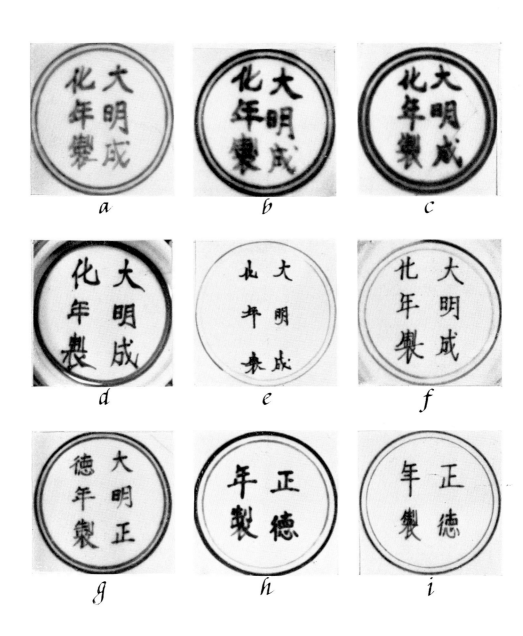

98A, B, C. CHʻÊNG HUA MARK AND PERIOD
D. CHʻÊNG HUA MARK, SECOND HALF SIXTEENTH CENTURY
E. CHʻÊNG HUA MARK, KʻANG HSI PERIOD
F. CHʻÊNG HUA MARK, YUNG CHÊNG PERIOD
G. CHÊNG TÊ MARK AND PERIOD, ʻMOHAMMEDANʼ WARE
H. CHÊNG TÊ MARK AND PERIOD
I. CHÊNG TÊ MARK AND PERIOD

See pages 75, 76

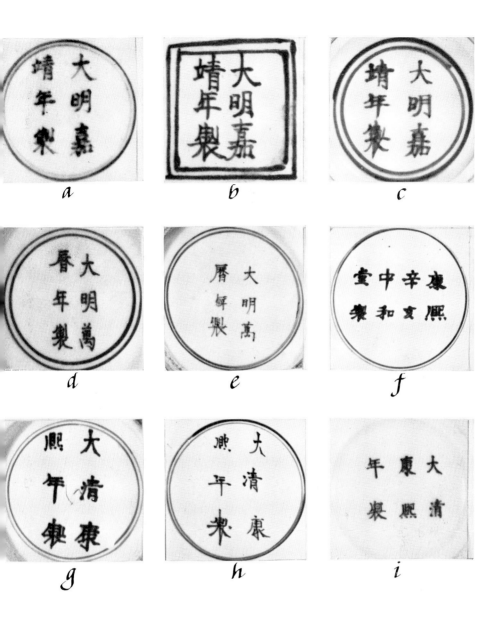

99A, B. CHIA CHING MARK AND PERIOD
C. CHIA CHING MARK, EARLY K'ANG HSI
D. WAN LI MARK AND PERIOD
E. WAN LI MARK, JAPANESE
F. EARLY K'ANG HSI MARK (DATED 1671)
G. EARLY K'ANG HSI MARK AND PERIOD
H. K'ANG HSI MARK AND PERIOD (MIDDLE PERIOD)
I. K'ANG HSI MARK AND PERIOD (LATE PERIOD)
See pages 75, 77

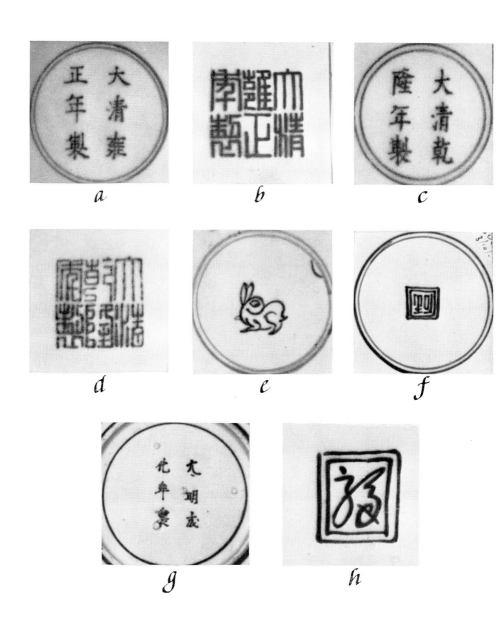

100A. YUNG CHÊNG MARK AND PERIOD

B. YUNG CHÊNG SEAL MARK AND PERIOD

C. CH'IEN LUNG MARK AND PERIOD

D. CH'IEN LUNG SEAL MARK AND PERIOD

E. 'HARE AND CRESCENT MOON' MARK, K'ANG HSI PERIOD

F. 'SHOP' MARK, K'ANG HSI PERIOD

G. CH'ÊNG HUA MARK, JAPANESE

H. *Fuku* MARK, JAPANESE

See pages 76, 77

8-11-72